Chatham House P

US Troops in Europe

Chatham House Papers · 25

US Troops in Europe

Phil Williams

To Eric

Very Best Wishes

Phil. Williams

The Royal Institute of International Affairs

Routledge & Kegan Paul
London, Boston and Henley

The Royal Institute of International Affairs is an unofficial body which promotes the scientific study of international questions and does not express opinions of its own. The opinions expressed in this paper are the responsibility of the author.

First published 1984
by Routledge & Kegan Paul Ltd
14 Leicester Square, London WC2H 7PH
9 Park Street, Boston, Mass. 02108, USA and
Broadway House, Newtown Road,
Henley-on-Thames, Oxon RG9 1EN
Set by Hope Services, Abingdon and
printed in Great Britain by
Billing & Son Ltd, Worcester

ISBN 0-7102-0422-1

Contents

Acknowledgments

This paper forms part of the Chatham House research project on US foreign policy and European interests which was funded by the Leverhulme Trust.

I would like to acknowledge a considerable debt to all the participants in the Chatham House study groups which met to discuss the paper. The comments, criticisms and suggestions from these meetings were invaluable. Thanks are also due to David Watt, the former director of Chatham House, who was a considerable help in the early stages of the work, and to the director of studies, William Wallace, who was a source of encouragement throughout. The director of Chatham House, Admiral Sir James Eberle, and John Roper offered numerous and incisive comments on the completed draft, for which I was extremely grateful. Joan Pearce was a great source of help and guidance throughout and played a major part in editing the final manuscript. My thanks are also due to Pauline Wickham, who oversaw the production of the paper with her customary skill and diligence.

Special mention must be made of the staff of the press library and the library at Chatham House. Their expertise and assistance made the research much easier. Thanks, too, to my other colleagues who helped to provide such a congenial atmosphere in which to work.

The final responsibility for the views and arguments expressed in the study, and for its shortcomings, is of course my own.

P.W.

1 Introduction

The American commitment to the security of Western Europe has been one of the most enduring features of the international order which emerged in the aftermath of the Second World War. It has also been one of the least controversial elements of American foreign policy, many other aspects of which have been the subject of considerable argument and debate. That the independence of Western Europe was, and is, important to the United States has rarely been denied. Much more controversial, however, has been the question of precisely how much the United States needs to do in order to ensure that West European security is maintained. More specifically, there has been considerable, if intermittent, argument about the size of the American military contingent deployed in Western Europe.

The decision to send troops to Europe precipitated the Great Debate of 1951, in which Senator Robert Taft and other Republicans argued that such a step would encourage the Europeans to depend excessively for their security on the United States. This criticism was echoed in the 1960s and 1970s by Senator Mike Mansfield, the Democratic Majority Leader, who suggested that a substantial cut in the number of US troops deployed in Western Europe would encourage the allies to shoulder a greater share of the burden and take responsibility for their own security. In the first half of the 1980s, there have been arguments for reducing the American military presence in Western Europe from critics as diverse as Senator Stevens of Alaska, Chairman of the Defense Appropriations Subcommittee; Jeffrey Record, an analyst at the Institute for Foreign Policy Analysis and a former staff assistant to Senator Sam Nunn; and Professor Irving Kristol, a prominent conservative spokesman. More surprising — and much more disconcerting to many Europeans — was the addition to the ranks of those advocating a fundamental change in the American contribution to NATO of former Secretary of State Henry Kissinger and Senator Sam Nunn of Georgia, one of the leading congressional authorities on military issues. Kissinger's views were expressed in *Time* magazine in March 1984,[1] and in June 1984 Nunn introduced legislation to bring about a 90,000 reduction in the American presence unless the allies did more for their own defence.

The Reagan Administration rejected these proposals. Not only did it publicly disavow Kissinger's arguments, but it also lobbied successfully against the Nunn Amendment. Nevertheless, the very fact that people of the stature of Kissinger and Nunn could contemplate such measures is highly significant. Both men played a key role in defeating congressional demands for troop reductions in the first half of the 1970s. Consequently, their demand for troop cuts is clearly symptomatic of a growing impatience in both congressional and public opinion with allies who, it is argued, have failed to bear a fair share of the defence burden.

Not surprisingly, the reaction of most European governments to these recent proposals has been one of apprehension. In the 1960s and 1970s, demands for even moderate cutbacks provoked unequivocal condemnation from West Europeans who were concerned that these would mean a weakening of the American commitment. The more sporadic debate of the 1980s has already aroused a similar response. John Nott, former UK Secretary of State for Defence, argued that it was not simply the number of American troops which was important, but the fact that a cut in troop levels would be seen as symbolic of a changed American approach to European security. As he stated, 'Any reduction which was perceived to cast doubt on the strength of the American commitment to Europe would serve only to weaken deterrence. It would be greatly welcomed by the Soviet Union, and the outcome could scarcely be in American interests.'[2] The response to Kissinger's and Nunn's arguments, that unless the European allies were prepared to strengthen their conventional forces the United States should substantially reduce its military presence in Europe, was very similar. Apart from the former German Chancellor, Helmut Schmidt, who acknowledged that a limited reduction of US troops from Europe 'would not necessarily be a misfortune', the formal reaction from most

West European governments and NATO officials was one of cautious but unequivocal condemnation of the idea.[3]

In addition, however, to this rather traditional, not to say predictable, European reaction to the idea of American troop cuts, there has been a more muted strand of opinion — symbolized in Schmidt's remarks — which accepts that limited reductions might have certain benefits, and in particular would jolt the Europeans into doing more to bolster their own security. Furthermore, it could be argued that such reductions would provide a degree of reassurance to the Soviet Union and would thereby contribute to a lessening of tension between East and West. To some extent this less alarmist approach is prompted by the belief that Western Europe remains closely associated with, and dependent upon, the United States at a time when neither the wisdom of this association nor the need for this dependence is any longer self-evident. Although the desire for a complete decoupling of Western Europe from the United States is confined to the more radical elements in European opinion, the belief that Western Europe should play a more independent role in determining its own destiny has considerably more support. While such sentiments can be attributed partly to a loss of faith in American leadership — which itself stems from a loss of faith in American leaders — they are also related to the growing conviction that the degree of dependence on the United States currently exhibited by Western Europe is no longer appropriate. Such dependence was inevitable in the immediate postwar period, but now that Western Europe has recovered economically, this is no longer the case. Consequently, it is increasingly argued that the states of Western Europe should be able to make appropriate dispositions for their own security. An asymmetrical alliance was both necessary and desirable in the 1950s and even the 1960s; in the 1980s it is both undesirable and unnecessary.

The point was put most graphically by Senator Mike Mansfield in the early 1970s, when he expressed astonishment at the fact that 'the 250 million people of Western Europe, with tremendous industrial resources and long military experience, are unable to organize an effective military coalition to defend themselves against 200 million Russians, who are contending at the same time with 800 million Chinese, but must continue after 20 years to depend upon 200 million Americans for their defence'.[4] More recently, Professor Hedley Bull has suggested that such dependence is undignified for nations as strong and stable as those of Western Europe.[5] In other words, the idea of minimizing European dependence on the United States stems from a mixture of fear and hope: fear about the direction in which American policies appear to be heading, and hope that Western Europe can either disengage from the superpower competition while still maintaining its security *vis-à-vis* the Soviet Union or, at the very least, play a more important role in NATO *vis-à-vis* the United States.

American troop reductions, therefore, could be a useful and important step towards the creation of a Western Europe which, if not entirely self-sufficient in security matters, would certainly be far less dependent on Washington than is currently the case. Such a transition will be difficult, but those who advocate it argue that the costs and dangers attendant on the *status quo* are even greater.

At the same time as the possibility of US troop reductions is once again being mooted, there is, somewhat paradoxically, increasing concern with strengthening conventional forces and thereby lessening NATO's dependence on nuclear weapons. A number of critics of NATO's existing posture have called for a 'no first use' strategy, whereby the Alliance formally renounces any intention to initiate the use of nuclear weapons in the event of hostilities in Europe.[6] Although this approach has been rejected by officials in the United States and Western Europe as too extreme, there does appear to be a growing consensus on the need for stronger conventional forces and 'no early first use'. It is argued that without such measures NATO will remain wedded to a strategy which lacks strategic credibility and political legitimacy. The danger is that it will neither deter the adversary nor reassure those whom it is designed to protect.[7]

The discussion about augmenting conventional forces has been cast partly in terms of increasing defence budgets, with General Rogers, NATO's Supreme Allied Commander in Europe, advocating a 4 per cent per annum real increase. More realistically, it has focused on the need to revise military tactics, and to make more efficient use of existing resources through national specialization of roles, common procurement and the like. Considerable attention has also been given to the possibility of exploiting existing and emerging technologies for roles and missions which have hitherto required the use of nuclear weapons. None of these approaches contemplates massive increases in conventional force levels, emphasizing instead the need to exploit more fully the resources already available. Nevertheless, it seems clear that substantial reductions in the American presence in Western Europe would hinder these efforts to give NATO's strategy of flexible response, which was adopted in 1967, the degree of flexibility and the variety of options its name implies.

In other words, there is a juxtaposition of two separate impulses in the current debate over European security. To the extent that threats of American troop reductions are intended to galvanize the European allies into devoting more resources to defence, then the approaches are complementary. Kissinger's comments and the Nunn Amendment can be seen in this light. But if the possibility of troop reductions is more than a bargaining device to encourage greater European burden-sharing, then it does threaten to undermine moves to strengthen NATO's conventional capabilities and, in this sense, is ultimately inconsistent with the discussions about enhanced defence.

Indeed, the very existence of these potentially competing strands suggests that the Atlantic Alliance needs to conduct a review of its strategic, military and political requirements for the remainder of the 1980s, the 1990s and the first decade of the next century. This would provide an opportunity for the West Europeans in particular to consider a number of issues:

(1) What is the most appropriate relationship between Western Europe and the United States in the future? Are there realistic alternatives to West European dependence on the United States, or is this rooted in geopolitical and strategic conditions which are not only immutable, but which obstruct any substantial alteration in existing security arrangements?

(2) How important is it to Western Europe and to the United States that the American military presence in Europe remain at or near the existing levels? Are numbers sacrosanct, or is there sufficient flexibility to permit cuts in American force levels without necessarily jeopardizing the existing political and strategic framework? What kind of reductions in the American presence could be undertaken before there is any serious diminution in West European and American security? How important are considerations of timing and compensation as opposed to the level of forces?

(3) What is the relationship between security concerns in Europe itself and the more ambiguous and less direct threats to security and stability which exist elsewhere? Will the Alliance have to move towards a tacit or even explicit division of labour, whereby the Europeans take the primary responsibility for defence and deterrence in Europe and leave the United States to look after Alliance interests outside the NATO area? Alternatively, are American and European interests outside Europe so divergent that even a tacit and informal attempt to extend the scope of Alliance concerns will merely place additional and possibly intolerable burdens on an Atlantic relationship that is already under considerable strain?

(4) How would reductions in the American military presence in Western Europe be received in Moscow? Is it the case, as some commentators assume, that the Soviet Union is anxious to see the United States disengage from Western Europe, and that limited troop reductions would, therefore, be welcomed as a step in the right direction? Alternatively, are there perhaps dangers in such an eventuality that might render it far less attractive to Soviet decision-makers than is often suggested?

(5) Finally, and even more fundamentally, what is the nature of the threat to Western Europe posed by the Soviet Union? Would a Soviet incursion into Western Europe be, as one American analyst has suggested, 'the most elaborately anticipated and least expected invasion in European history'?[8] Is Soviet adventurism in Europe likely to result from opportunity or only from need?[9] Closely related to these issues are questions about the most appropriate mix of policies for NATO to pursue towards Moscow. Deterrence and defence may be necessary conditions of West European security, but are they sufficient? To what extent do military preparations need to be supplemented by dialogue and cooperation with the Soviet Union and its allies? How much emphasis should be placed on reassurance through confidence-building measures, arms control, economic interchanges and the like?

Many of these questions, of course, transcend the issue of American troops in Europe and go to the heart of the postwar security arrangements in Europe and the division of the continent into rival spheres of interest. Yet the American military presence is itself a manifestation of this division, and of the fact that Western Europe has been unable to provide for its own defence. US troops deployed in Western Europe are the visible evidence that there is no indigenous countervailing power to offset Soviet preponderance. They are also symbolic of the American willingness to fight on Europe's behalf in the event of Soviet aggression. Memories of the First and Second World Wars, when the United States initially remained aloof, appear to confirm the need for tangible guarantees. In the light of all this, it is perhaps understandable that the Europeans are reluctant to contemplate any change in the *status quo*. Certainly, substantial reductions in the American presence would confront all West European governments, especially that of the Federal Republic of Germany, with difficult and unpalatable choices they would prefer to avoid.

Nevertheless, there may be more flexibility in the current arrangements than is generally assumed. It is conceivable that the precise number of American troops is less important than is often asserted, and that the Europeans are in danger of endowing limited changes with unlimited significance, and creating a self-fulfilling prophecy. If the existing number of troops is regarded as sacrosanct, then even relatively modest reductions might be interpreted as the prelude to a removal of the security commitment, which might in turn encourage the allies to adopt a more accommodating stance towards Moscow and add further to American disillusionment. The implication is that the Europeans need a more critical attitude towards their own fears.

In other words, the issues outlined above need to be analysed in a way which does not simply reiterate the conventional wisdom with its emphasis on maintaining the *status quo*. It has been argued, for example, that 'any unilateral withdrawal of US forces, of any magnitude, and according to any timetable, would signal to both the Soviets and the West Germans that the United States was taking the first step in the process of decreasing and eventually liquidating its absolute security guarantee to Western Europe'.[10] Why this should be so is not self-evident. No security guarantee can be absolute: it can merely be stronger or weaker. Once this is acknowledged, it requires little imagination to suggest that a more discriminating approach to the question of American troop reductions is also required. Why, for example, should such a move be regarded as the first step towards liquidating the American commitment, rather than as a sensible act of military regrouping or an attempt to ensure that the deployment of troops has continued political support in the United States? A leaner but highly combat-efficient force might be preferable to a larger contingent with a high ratio of support forces to combat forces. What kind of units or personnel are withdrawn, therefore, may be as important as the numbers involved. Similarly, a smaller presence which is politically robust, in the sense that it attracts less criticism, may be preferable to a larger troop contingent which is more visible and more controversial.

The issues are not clear-cut. Furthermore, the juxtaposition of suggestions for withdrawing American troops with proposals for strengthening NATO's conventional forces implies that there is, potentially at least, more fluidity in European security arrangements than there has been for some time. The fact that challenges to the *status quo* are coming from a variety of directions would support this contention.

Before examining some of the possible changes and how they might be handled, the paper considers the historical background to the American military presence in Europe, and attempts to explain why this presence has often been controversial. This is done in Chapter 2. Chapter 3 analyses the presence itself in terms of its size, composition, cost and rationale. Having spelt out the existing situation in some detail, the pressures for change are identified in Chapter 4. Chapter 5 considers options involving strengthened conventional capabilities, while Chapter 6 examines the consequences of reductions in the US military presence. It assesses not only the scope of possible troop cuts, but also the possibility of compensatory measures being undertaken by the European allies. The final chapter outlines the main conclusions and recommendations of the study.

Throughout the work, the main focus is on the size and shape of the US forces in Europe; but this should be seen as part of the broader questions concerning the American commitment, Alliance strategy, and the sharing of burdens and responsibilities. Furthermore, when considering and evaluating the different options, attention has to be given to the criteria on which a stable peace in Europe can be maintained in the years ahead. In other words, although the focus of the study appears to be rather narrow, it has to cover much broader issues which go to the core of the Atlantic relationship. Questions about US troops in Europe are also questions about the viability of extended deterrence; about the future of European-American relations; about the most appropriate arrangements for maintaining and enhancing stability in Europe; and, indeed, about the very nature of security itself.

2 The background

In 1949, the US Secretary of State, Dean Acheson, was asked whether or not the United States was expecting to send a substantial number of troops to Europe on a more or less permanent basis. He replied that the answer was a clear and absolute no![1] In 1950, as part of its response to the concerns precipitated by the Korean War, the Truman Administration reversed its position on this question and decided to send four divisions to Europe to join the two already there on occupation duties. In fiscal year 1982, the American presence in Europe numbered over 350,000 men.[2] Perhaps even more significant was the admission by Under-Secretary of State for Political Affairs Lawrence Eagleburger, before the Senate Committee on Foreign Relations in November 1982, that 'to some degree and in some force' the United States would 'have to be in Europe through the rest of the century'.[3] This comment was based on the premise that the United States is involved in Europe not out of altruism, but because of its own self-interest. It was also a recognition of the fact that, for the European allies, the United States military presence has taken on enormous significance: it is widely regarded as the most important manifestation of the American commitment and as the key to the maintenance of peace and security on the Central Front. Indeed, any suggestion that the United States might reduce the level of its forces immediately provokes great anxieties in European capitals – especially Bonn – that such stirrings represent a weakening of the American commitment. The American military presence on more or less its existing scale is regarded by most governments and defence ministries in Western Europe as essential to the maintenance of the Western Alliance itself.

The importance now attached to the American presence in Europe is somewhat ironic in view of the initial assumptions about the Atlantic Alliance set out in the North Atlantic Treaty of 1949.[4] The Alliance was seen almost exclusively as a 'guarantee pact', which would reassure the West Europeans about their security and thereby provide the climate of confidence which was necessary to encourage the level of economic investment required to bring the Marshall Plan to fruition. It was also believed that it would draw the line in Europe and convey to the Soviet Union that any move against Western Europe would involve conflict with the United States which, when the Treaty was signed and ratified, still had a monopoly of atomic weapons. This is not to suggest that there was a serious expectation that the Soviet Union intended to launch an attack on Western Europe. Although there had been anxieties about the possibility of war in the early months of 1948 (prompted by the coup in Czechoslovakia and Soviet pressure on Norway), by the middle of 1949 these had subsided. The threat was seen as being primarily political in nature and one which stemmed from the lack of countervailing power on the European continent itself. Only the explicit involvement of the United States could restore this balance and ensure that the Soviet Union did not extend its influence into Western Europe as it had done (although under very different circumstances) in Eastern Europe.

This is not to deny that there was some concern over the military threat. Indeed, the West Europeans and the United States felt it necessary to draw up contingency plans for countering an incursion into Western Europe by the Soviet Union. From the outset, the Alliance members recognized that there would be a common strategic concept in the event of an attack. Furthermore, immediately after the approval of the North Atlantic Treaty by the Senate, the Truman Administration introduced its proposals for military assistance to Western Europe. The purpose of the Military Assistance Programme was to enable the allies to develop substantial military forces of their own. It was hoped that this would enable the United States to limit its direct involvement in the defence of Western Europe.

The desire to limit American participation was also apparent in the notion of a division of labour which provided the framework for military planning. According to this, the United States was to supply the strategic and tactical air power, and the European allies, especially France, were to provide the ground forces. Furthermore, the build-up of these forces was to take second place to the needs of economic recovery. In other words, in the twelve months following the signing of the North Atlantic Treaty, it was assumed that American involvement in the defence of Europe would be carefully circumscribed, and that West European efforts could afford to be leisurely and long-term rather than urgent and immediate.[5]

The idea that American participation in West European security arrangements should be limited remained in the foreground throughout the late 1940s and early 1950s. Indeed, the Marshall Plan and the Military Assistance Programme were both part of an attempt to restore Western Europe to a position in which it would be able to look after its own security without continued dependence on the United States.[6] The American security commitment was regarded by many legislators as essentially an emergency measure made necessary by the weakness of the West European states – weakness which was regarded as a temporary consequence of the Second World War, rather than as part of a more fundamental shift in the balance of power. But even this circumscribed involvement was a dramatic departure for a nation steeped in a diplomatic tradition which had always viewed entangling alliances with suspicion and disdain. Throughout the late 1940s, the Truman Administration had to contend with a small but powerful band of senators who vigorously opposed its policy towards Western Europe. It was partly in an attempt to placate the critics that administration spokesmen during the hearings on the North Atlantic Treaty and the Military Assistance Programme emphasized the importance of European self-help. American security assistance, like American economic aid, was to decline as the European allies regained their self-reliance and rebuilt their military strength.

Most of these assumptions and calculations changed dramatically as the result of the outbreak of war in Korea in June 1950. Although the war had little direct relevance to the situation in Europe, it challenged the prevailing consensus on both the nature of the Soviet threat and the actions required to contain it – especially as the invasion of South Korea came less than a year after the Soviet Union had succeeded in ending America's monopoly of atomic weapons. The parallels between divided Korea and divided Germany, together with the belief that the North Korean attack might be a feint to divert American attention and leave the way open for a Soviet move against Western Europe, cast doubt upon the effectiveness of the American security guarantee to the European allies, and prompted the Truman Administration to make a far-reaching reassessment of the requirements of Atlantic security. As a result, the Alliance was transformed from a unilateral guarantee pact to a collective defence organization. Not only was West European rearmament deemed essential, but, if Soviet conventional power was to be offset, it was argued in Washington that this rearmament process had to include the Federal Republic of Germany. Indeed, the Joint Chiefs of Staff insisted that if US troops were to be sent to Europe, this could be done only as part of a package deal which also included the creation of a unified command and the removal of the constraints on German rearmament.[7] Without these other steps, they argued, the deployment of US troops would be an act of military folly and, in the event of a Soviet attack, would lead to either the destruction or the evacuation of the American contingent.

The decision to send four divisions to Europe and to initiate German rearmament fundamentally transformed the nature of the conflict in Europe. What had hitherto been primarily a political and diplomatic struggle, albeit one with military overtones, became first and foremost a military confrontation. Yet the traditional concerns about 'entangling alliances' remained. These were particularly strong in the Senate, and during the first three months of 1951, Republican senators led by Robert Taft and Kenneth Wherry challenged not only the strategic rationale but also the constitutional propriety of Truman's decision. At the end of what became known as the Great Debate, the Senate finally acquiesced in the President's policy and passed Resolution 99. Although this resolution upheld the deployment policy, it also made clear that if more troops were to be sent in the future, the President would be expected to seek congressional approval. Furthermore, the Great Debate had revealed that the presence of US troops in Europe was inherently controversial, departing as it did from all the traditional precepts and practices of American foreign policy. Administration spokesmen were acutely aware of this, and during the Senate hearings on the troops to Europe decision they emphasized that the American action would improve European morale and encourage the allies in their own rearmament efforts. General Eisenhower, the first Supreme Allied Commander Europe (SACEUR), also made clear that his long-term objective was to minimize the American contribution and maximize that of the allies. Although other officials such as Dean Acheson may have thought differently, Eisenhower certainly regarded the US presence in Europe as a temporary one, based on the need to provide a breathing space, during which the Europeans could rebuild their own defence establishments. Although changed circumstances meant that the United States was now participating in West European defence much more directly than had been anticipated a year earlier, the idea of a diminishing scale of involvement (rather like the Marshall Plan) still remained a central element in the thinking of some officials.

As President, Eisenhower had the opportunity to bring the breathing space to an end. He apparently wanted to make substantial cuts in the US contingent, but was dissuaded from doing so by advisers who argued that the time was inappropriate and the matter too delicate.[8] It was not entirely surprising, therefore, that in the early 1960s there were grumblings from the Senate about the continued drain on American resources caused by the deployment. What was perhaps more unexpected was that the leading figures in this were not the conservative Republicans who had been most vociferous in their opposition to sending troops in 1951, but Democratic Senators Mike Mansfield and Stuart Symington, both of whom had impeccable credentials as internationalists.

The pressure for a reappraisal began in the early 1960s, but became much more serious in 1966, when Majority Leader Mansfield introduced a Sense of the Senate Resolution, which recommended that the Executive branch initiate a substantial reduction of US forces in Europe. Although Mansfield never put this resolution to the vote, he gathered an increasing number of co-sponsors, and from 1966 to 1970 was able – intermittently at least – to exert considerable pressure on the Johnson and Nixon Administrations to reduce the presence in Europe.

There were several considerations which contributed to the growing support for Mansfield's proposals during these years. One of these was the widespread perception that the European allies were not making military contributions commensurate with their new-found economic strength. Burden-sharing concerns had been evident from the inception of the Alliance, and had led the United States to insist on the principle of European self-help as a prerequisite of continued American assistance.

The Europeans, however, appeared reluctant to do anything which would make an American disengagement possible, and, on most indicators of relative effort, they appeared to be lagging well behind the United States. At the same time, they were extremely critical of American policy elsewhere, especially Vietnam. Although Mansfield's desire for troop reductions in Europe predated the deepening of US involvement in Vietnam, he undoubtedly obtained considerable support from those Senators who felt that the US had become over-committed; that the NATO allies had been backward in their support for American efforts in South-East Asia; and that the military presence in Europe was consequently the most appropriate target for retrenchment. Furthermore, in the late 1960s and the early 1970s there was considerable concern about the opportunity costs of the American military presence overseas. Many liberals in particular felt that American foreign policy had become too militarized, with the result that it was diverting funds from domestic social welfare programmes. And once again the most appropriate area for savings appeared to be manpower deployed overseas.

An additional incentive for a reduction in the American presence in Europe was that it would have balance-of-payment savings. Throughout the 1960s, there was considerable concern over the dollar drain associated with the troop contingent in Germany.[9] And although the Federal Republic agreed to compensate Washington with substantial offset payments, these were not always deemed sufficient. Indeed, some of the arrangements of the late 1960s proved particularly unpopular. As part of the offset agreements of 1967 and 1968, Bonn purchased medium-term treasury bonds from the United States. Although this was of immediate benefit to the US balance of payments, Washington had ultimately to redeem the bonds and meanwhile pay interest in order to keep its own troops in Germany. What made this all the more galling for many Senators was the fact that by this stage Western Europe, and especially the Federal Republic, had already emerged as a major economic competitor of the United States. In these circumstances there was far less tolerance for what appeared to be inequalities of effort and sacrifice between Washington and its European allies. These inequalities seemed more substantial than ever after the French decision of 1966 to withdraw from the integrated military structure of NATO. And although France was exploiting the increased freedom of manoeuvre provided by the growth of East-West détente in the aftermath of the Cuban missile crisis, de Gaulle's stance almost inevitably encouraged American Senators to demand a similar freedom for the United States. Mansfield, for example, argued that Washington should not take the security of Western Europe more seriously than the Europeans themselves. It was not coincidental that the Mansfield Resolution was first introduced in 1966, only a few months after de Gaulle announced his plans for withdrawal.

Although Mansfield appealed to the traditional, if latent, suspicion of Europe that had characterized American isolationism, he found it difficult to move the Executive branch. The Johnson Administration did agree to a limited redeployment of forces back to the United States as a result of the trilateral negotiations with London and Bonn in late 1966 and early 1967, but the Nixon Administration was far more resistant to the pressure from the Senate. President Nixon used the congressional demands for reductions to underline the need for the Europeans to undertake a greater share of the burdens of defence. Nevertheless, he was not amenable to Mansfield's suggestion, and in December 1970 gave a commitment to the allies that there would be no immediate cut in US forces in Europe. The result was a more serious attempt by Mansfield to introduce legislation mandating, as opposed to recommending, troop reductions. From 1971, the proposals were no longer relatively innocuous resolutions which expressed the Sense of the Senate but were not legally binding, but amendments which, if they survived the legislative process, would have the force of law. Mansfield's efforts precipitated a series of votes on the Senate floor in May and November 1971, but they failed to achieve their end.

In 1973, however, the pressure was more intense than ever before, and on 26 September a Mansfield Amendment to cut troops in Europe actually passed the Senate, only to be reversed the same afternoon, when a parliamentary technicality required a second vote and gave the administration an opportunity to engage in a short but highly effective lobbying campaign. By 1974, the high point of sentiment in favour of a smaller troop contingent in Western Europe had passed, and another Mansfield Amendment was defeated quite comfortably. By the mid-1970s it appeared that the issue had become a dead one. With Mansfield's departure from the Senate, there was no obvious successor as leader of a troop-withdrawal coalition, and the congressional pressure was dismissed

as an aberration resulting from Mansfield's own very idiosyncratic out-
look and the peculiar circumstances of America in the early 1970s when
the excesses of Vietnam and the neglect of domestic needs had provoked
indiscriminate demands for far-reaching military retrenchment.

Consequently, the revival of congressional concern with the issue at
the beginning of the 1980s caught many observers in both Western
Europe and the United States by surprise. In many ways, however, the
resurgence of interest in the idea of troop reductions was a predictable
reaction to the resentment felt in the United States about what was
widely interpreted as a failure of the allies to fulfil their part of the
transatlantic bargain and shoulder an equitable share of the defence
burden. Part of it of course was tactical: threatening to reduce American
forces in Europe is one way of attempting to get the allies to do more.
Yet to dismiss congressional actions as simply an exercise in alliance
bargaining would be a mistake. Although 'the Congress has accepted
fully the American commitment to NATO, it never has accepted the
indefinite presence of large contingents of American forces in Europe.'[10]
It is hardly surprising, therefore, that this presence frequently has to be
justified in terms of its contribution to American security and the much
greater financial costs likely to be incurred if the United States had to
do without its European allies. Indeed, it is not coincidental that the
rationale for the US military presence in Western Europe was developed
most fully and explicitly during the debates over the Mansfield Amendments, when the challenge to the *status quo* was at its strongest. The
most recent debate has provided one or two variations on familiar
themes, but has added little that is new or different: the rationale for
maintaining the existing level of American forces in Europe was more
or less the same in 1983 and 1984 as it had been in 1973 and 1974.
And it is this rationale which must now be identified in more detail.

3 The military presence in Europe

The presence

The American military presence in Europe is an explicit acknowledgment of the importance attached in Washington to the maintenance of West European security. As one recent study noted, the United States maintains in the Federal Republic 'a force equivalent to almost 6 divisions. The United States has further committed itself to a capability for sending 6 more divisions within two weeks of a decision to reinforce. The active and reserve forces contain another 14 divisions and 21 brigades, maintained principally to back up the forward-deployed forces and early reinforcements.'[1] In addition, there are 7 Air Force fighter wings forward-deployed, which in a crisis would be rapidly reinforced by another 20 Air Force wings from the United States. The Sixth Fleet in the Mediterranean and the Second Fleet in the Atlantic are further manifestations of the American commitment and the importance attached to both forward deployments and the capacity for reinforcement and resupply in the event of hostilities.

Although these ground, air and naval forces have a considerable capacity for conventional defence, their nuclear components are both tactically and strategically important. This continues to be the case despite the growth of concern over the role of battlefield nuclear weapons in any conflict in Europe. In 1979, it was decided to reduce the number of US battlefield nuclear weapons deployed in Europe by 1,000. In October 1983, NATO announced a further reduction of 1,400 warheads to be carried out over several years. Yet, even after this withdrawal, over 4,500 battlefield weapons will remain in Europe. Furthermore, the concepts of operations of the American forces deployed on the Continent are based on the assumption that in any major conflict these weapons would almost certainly have to be used. As one analyst has observed, 'the most striking feature . . . is the extent to which all services, and nearly all branches of services, have been nuclearized'.[2] If this is a further indication of the importance attached to the security of Western Europe, so too is the size of the American contingent.

The number of military personnel actually deployed in Europe at the end of fiscal year 1982 was about 356,000: about 256,000 in the Federal Republic, 67,000 elsewhere in Europe, and 33,000 afloat.[3] These numbers represent an increase of some 40–50,000 since the mid-1970s, when the congressional pressure for reductions subsided. Yet this is not entirely surprising, since, from the 1950s onwards, there have periodically been variations in the level of US forces forward-deployed in Europe going well beyond the normal fluctuations associated with changing operational requirements.

The high point of the American presence came in 1953, when the total of personnel in Europe reached 427,000. After declining by almost 50,000 throughout the rest of the 1950s, the number peaked again at 417,000 as the result of the Berlin crisis of 1961. In the aftermath of this confrontation, there was a sharp decline as the temporary reinforcements were withdrawn. Nevertheless, there were still 360,000 men in Europe in the mid-1960s. The demands of the Vietnam War, however, took a considerable toll, and in 1970 and 1971 the number fell below 300,000. After hovering around 300,000 to 313,000 in the first half of the 1970s, the number increased to a level which, though still far removed from the high points, is greater than at any time since the mid-1960s.[4] The rationale for maintaining forces on this scale in Western Europe must now be examined, after which the costs of the presence can be assessed.

The rationale

The rationale for maintaining a substantial military presence in Western Europe has changed in certain respects since the troops to Europe decision of September 1950. Yet the strands of continuity are, if anything, even more striking than the changes. The deployment of the troops was undertaken in accordance with the precepts of the containment strategy. Many of those precepts seem to be as important in the Reagan Administration's foreign policy as they were in Truman's, and, as a result of the growth of Soviet military power, the notion of containing Soviet expansionism has taken on more rather than less significance. Although Europe was the initial focus of a strategy that has since been extended to other areas, the Continent is still regarded by many observers as not only the main theatre of the Cold War, but also as the main prize. If containment fails in Europe, the prospects for success elsewhere are remote. Even though the Reagan Administration has replaced the predominantly European orientation of the Carter Administration with a global perspective reliant upon an expanded navy and the Rapid Deployment Force, it still acknowledges that Western Europe is the first line of America's defence. As one State Department official explained to the Senate Committee on Foreign Relations in 1982: 'Europe has become more not less important for us over the three decades since the Alliance was formed. The European and American economies are now so tightly knit together that neither can grow without the other. The allied countries are our main export market. American direct investment in Europe is an important positive factor in our balance of payments and contributes heavily to the profitability of American business.

'The United States and Western Europe are more than simply trading and political partners, however. Our security is unalterably linked with theirs. Western Europe is quite literally our first line of defense. It is the center of our global competition with the Soviet Union and by far the most alluring object of Soviet ambitions.'[5] Implicit in this statement was a recognition that without strong allies in Western Europe – either because of the growth of neutralism or because of the domination of the Continent by the Soviet Union – the global competition with Moscow would become far more difficult and costly for the United States. The American commitment to Western Europe provides allies, bases, and real estate in the event of hostilities; it also denies the Soviet Union access to the material and industrial resources of the West Europeans. In other words, compelling geopolitical and geostrategic realities make an American commitment to the security of Western Europe as important in the 1980s as it was in the 1940s and 1950s, or, for that matter, in the two World Wars.

The presence of American troops contributes to the security of Western Europe and the United States in several ways. Perhaps the most important of these is that it conveys to the Soviet Union American interest and intent: interest in keeping Western Europe free from Soviet domination, and intent to respond with force in the event of Soviet trespassing on these interests. Even though the emergence of strategic parity has raised enormous question marks over the American nuclear guarantee to Western Europe – in that it would be suicidal and consequently irrational for the United States to respond to Soviet conventional aggression with nuclear retaliation – the presence of American troops (together with the more recent deployment of cruise missiles and Pershing IIs) provides a crucial link to American strategic forces. The troops no longer represent a tripwire leading almost automatically to massive retaliation, as they apparently did in the 1950s. Nevertheless, they provide an assured American response, thereby raising the spectre of a direct Soviet–American clash with all the potential for escalation that this involves. Merely by their presence in Europe, American forces commit Washington to a process which could be so irrational and uncontrollable that nuclear war might be the eventual outcome, even though both sides are anxious to avoid it. Escalation can occur inadvertently as well as through deliberate decisions, and it is this possibility which shores up the credibility of the American nuclear guarantee to Western Europe in an era of nuclear parity. As McGeorge Bundy noted in 1979, what makes deterrence in Europe effective is 'the very evident risk that any large-scale engagement between Soviet and American forces would rapidly and uncontrollably become general, nuclear and disastrous.'[6]

As well as their contribution to peacetime deterrence through the potential link to American strategic capabilities, the troops in Europe make an important contribution to NATO's capacity for forward defence and flexible response. The move from massive retaliation to flexible response gave the American presence a new role. Instead of being merely a tripwire, the troops became a crucial part of what was hoped would be a stalwart conventional posture, capable of denying the Warsaw Pact outright victory and, it was hoped, even limited territorial gain. Although such a prospect had hitherto been regarded as fanciful, the revised estimates of the conventional military balance in Central Europe which emerged from the Office of Systems Analysis in the Department of

Defense during the mid-1960s suggested that it was at least within the bounds of possibility.[7] Although the assessments of analysts such as Alain Enthoven were not accepted by the Joint Chiefs of Staff as a reliable guide to the European balance, they nevertheless gave some credence to the idea that in the event of an attack the prospects for NATO were not as dismal as had often been assumed.

This is not to deny that NATO would face formidable difficulties in its efforts to contain a large-scale attack by Soviet forces, especially if the Soviet Union had obtained the advantage of either tactical or strategic surprise. Many observers believe that Warsaw Pact forces have significant but not overwhelming superiority over those of NATO, and this tends to strengthen the rationale for maintaining American troops at a fairly high level of readiness and at more or less the existing level. If the prospects for conventional defence were either completely hopeless or extremely good, then the arguments for reducing troops on the grounds of futility on the one hand or redundancy on the other would be overwhelming. As it is, there are sufficient imponderables in the Central European military equation for NATO to have a reasonable expectation that the forces deployed in the Federal Republic, together with reserves and reinforcements from Western Europe and the United States, would prevent a rapid and decisive Soviet victory. Question marks about the reliability of East European armies; uncertainties about the ratio of offensive to defensive forces required to ensure a breakthrough; arguments about quantity versus quality; differing assumptions about the length of political warning-time that NATO could realistically expect; and divergent assessments of the impact of fears of nuclear pre-emption render categorical judgments about the likely outcome of hostilities highly suspect.[8] The implication, though, is that the balance is sufficiently close for reductions in the American presence to be debilitating. With the existing level of American combat forces, NATO has some hope of mounting a sustained conventional defence; with significantly lower levels, these hopes would be undermined. This argument is particularly compelling at a time when the Alliance is attempting to minimize its dependence on nuclear weapons and move from deterrence through threats of escalation to a posture based upon the possibility of a successful conventional defence.

Closely related to this is the contribution made by the American contingent to political reassurance of the allies. The forces in place on the Continent provide manifest evidence of American support for the allies and essentially act as hostages to ensure that, in the event of aggression, the United States fulfils its obligations under Article 5 of the North Atlantic Treaty. Abandoning Western Europe in an emergency or a crisis is a far less feasible option if it also means abandoning a large number of American troops.

However, the justification for retaining the existing level of American forces in Europe does not rest exclusively upon the positive contribution they make. Equally salient are the predictions of the negative conse-quences that would ineluctably follow any reduction. In some ways, these arguments are merely variations on the themes just outlined: if the current level of US forces is essential for deterrence, defence and reassurance, reducing these forces will weaken deterrence, undermine the prospects for sustained defence and erode political confidence. In other ways, though, the arguments go beyond this and reveal how the *status quo* has taken on a sanctity and apparent immutability which are regarded by critics as evidence of bureaucratic inertia and political timidity, but which are seen by more sympathetic observers as a neces-sary continuation of policies which have been highly successful.

The first argument is that a troop reduction would convey the wrong signals to adversaries and allies alike. Under-Secretary of State Eagle-burger, for example, has suggested that such a move would have a far-reaching effect on the perceptions and calculations of the Soviet leaders, and expressed concern that 'if they see an America drawing inward, a demoralized Western Alliance and our European partners in doubt about the US commitment, their incentive to act with greater restraint will be diminished'.[9] The Soviet propensity both to take risks and to become more assertive in its dealings with Western Europe would be significantly increased. And, on the European side, the loss of confidence in the US guarantee would render most governments highly susceptible to such pressures.

It is argued further that such an effect could occur irrespective of the number of troops actually removed from Europe. As John Nott stated, 'it is not only numbers but the perception of change which is important',[10] and it seems to be widely assumed that even minor cuts by the United States would be interpreted as the beginnings of a more general American retreat from Europe. Even if this is dismissed as an exaggeration, there is a less apocalyptic and probably more persuasive argument that a cutback by the United States would have a reverse multiplier effect on NATO force levels. Not only would reductions initiated by Washington undermine the will of the allies to augment conventional forces, but they would also legitimize a general slackening of effort. American anxieties about the Soviet threat would no longer be taken seriously by the West Europeans, and the warnings that Washington has been sounding in recent years would be dismissed as simply a means of encouraging greater burden-sharing by the allies.

While these fears are obviously serious, they also represent the latest in a long line of arguments to the effect that the time is wrong for such a move. There is nearly always an issue on the current agenda which makes troop reductions appear somewhat inopportune. In the mid-1950s, when Eisenhower wanted to pull back some of his forces, his advisers convinced him that it would have an adverse impact on the Federal Republic, which was in the process of rearming. In 1974 the changes which had recently taken place in West European governments were cited as reasons for the Senate not to mandate troop cuts. In the early 1980s, there are again circumstances which militate against troop reductions. Not the least of these is the belief that a reduction of conventional forces which coincides with the deployment of cruise missiles and Pershing IIs would add credence to the claims of the peace movement that the United States is planning to wage a limited nuclear war in Europe. Actions which appear to increase NATO's dependence on nuclear weapons would merely intensify and give substance to such fears.

Another, less convincing, argument against troop cuts is that they would undermine the prospects for agreement in the Vienna talks on Mutual and Balanced Force Reductions. There is something rather spurious about this contention, given the glacier-like progress that was made in the negotiations during their first eleven years. The argument may have appeared a compelling one during the Mansfield debates of the late 1960s and early 1970s, but it has now ceased to have much credibility. Indeed, an examination of the history of the negotiations suggests that they were primarily a device to prevent unilateral American reductions resulting from congressional action. Apart from this somewhat bogus argument, however, the case for maintaining the existing number is not one that can be easily dismissed. The *status quo*, for all its short-comings, cannot be tampered with lightly. The importance attached by successive administrations in Washington to the American presence emerges clearly from even a brief consideration of the economic costs of maintaining it. And it is these costs which must now be examined.

The costs

Cost estimates regarding the American contribution to NATO are in-herently imprecise, since it is far from clear what forces should or should not be included. This emerged very clearly in the Defense Department's response to a question from Senator Sam Nunn during authorization hearings before the Senate Armed Services Committee in 1981. Although the Department provided a useful compilation of figures covering every fiscal year from 1974 to 1982, it acknowledged the difficulties at the outset: 'A precise total cost for NATO forces cannot be provided since most force elements have more than one purpose, and, in any major confrontation with the Warsaw Pact, all US forces that could contribute would be made available. Because almost everything in the defense budget contributes to the US commitment to NATO in one way or another, it is really not possible to separate NATO and non-NATO costs. By the same token, some of the forces formally "committed" to NATO might be employed elsewhere if contingencies arose at a time when NATO was not under attack.'[11]

One of the difficulties hinted at in this statement is whether a pro-portion of the cost of American strategic forces should be included in the estimate. Although the size of the strategic forces has to be seen primarily in relation to those of the Soviet Union (and to the desire to maintain 'essential equivalence' of both options and capabilities), the needs of extended deterrence have had considerable impact on the shape and size of the US arsenal. Even without this complication, there are some difficult issues. What proportion of the cost of United States General Purpose Forces is attributable solely to the commitment to Europe? If the commitment did not exist, would the forces simply be demobilized, or would they have other rationales, roles and missions?

One way of dealing with these problems is to distinguish between the American contribution to NATO and the American presence in Europe. The American contribution covers much more than the deployment in the European theatre; it takes into account not only forces based in the United States and earmarked for early reinforcement to Europe, but also those forces earmarked for later reinforcement. The estimates provided for Senator Nunn make such a breakdown, and on the basis of these figures the following points seem particularly salient:

(1) The $31.5 billion which was the cost of the forces actually deployed in Europe in fiscal year 1982 consisted of just over 16 per cent of total obligational authority for that year.

(2) If the forces assigned to the early reinforcement mission are also included, the cost jumps to $72.6 billion, which is almost 37 per cent of total outlays. If the later reinforcements are added, the cost is around $115.2 billion, or almost 59 per cent of outlays.

(3) The cost of the European deployment is well over double that of American forces in Asia. If there is a move towards the Pacific, therefore, it will merely go some way towards correcting what some critics would argue is an imbalance in favour of the European theatre.

(4) The manpower costs of American forces deployed in Europe, which for fiscal year 1982 was put at $8.4 billion, comprise just over 20 per cent of the total personnel cost (excluding the figure for retired pay) of $41.2 billion.

(5) These percentages have been fairly constant throughout the 1970s. Forces deployed in Europe in fiscal year 1974, for example, took 15.6 per cent of the defence budget, a figure only marginally below that for fiscal year 1982.

(6) When some proportion of the cost of strategic nuclear forces is also taken into account and later reinforcements (which are also earmarked for other contingencies) are excluded, it appears that the commitment to Europe consumes somewhere between 40 and 50 per cent of the American defence budget.

All this indicates that US defence policy and planning are primarily geared to the European theatre, a fact that was further emphasized in July 1984, when details were leaked of two separate assessments of US spending on the defence of Europe, one produced by the Department of Defense, and the other by the General Accounting Office. The Pentagon study, entitled 'United States Expenditures in Support of NATO', reportedly concluded that 58 per cent of the US defence budget for fiscal year 1985 was allocated to European defence, while forces actually deployed in Europe accounted for 18 per cent of the budget. The analysis produced by the General Accounting Office and based on figures for fiscal year 1982 concluded that forces committed to NATO (including a share of strategic nuclear forces) made up 56 per cent of the defence budget.[12]

The implication is that if major changes are to be brought about in the American defence budget, it will be necessary, if not to abandon the American commitment to Europe, at least to alter drastically the way in which this commitment is implemented. Controlling the defence budget may be impossible without reducing very substantially the American presence in Europe *and* reducing the size of the US Army. Bringing the forces back from Europe would not on its own yield budgetary savings of the scale necessary to change the direction of the American defence effort or to ease the overall deficit in the federal budget, unless the returned forces were also demobilized. Indeed, there would be substantial relocation costs associated with the simple removal of forces back from Europe to the United States. In April 1982, the Pentagon provided figures on these costs for the Senate Subcommittee on Defence Appropriations. One conclusion of what was admittedly an interim and not entirely neutral estimate was that the recall of all American ground forces and land-based tactical air-power would result in additional five-year costs of $17 billion. If one division only and its tactical air support were withdrawn, the restationing costs would amount to $0.8 billion over 5 years, but if circumstances demanded an airlift and fast sealift to send the division back to the Federal Republic, then the cost increase would rise to over $5 billion over the same period.[13]

Although there are grounds for some scepticism regarding the assumption that there would be no commensurate savings (if only of what in the early 1970s was described as the incremental costs of stationing forces in Europe), the high costs are not entirely surprising, especially in relation to total withdrawal. As the Department of Defense estimate noted: 'We are talking of moving and relocating about one third of our active Air Force and Army tactical forces from the bases where they have been permanently stationed for 37 years. This would involve a massive movement of men and material (e.g. 800,000 tons of Army ammunition), not to speak of rethinking our entire NATO strategy.'[14]

While the memorandum to the Subcommittee appears convincing, it is also somewhat artificial in the sense that no consideration was given to options which involved not only return of forces but also their subsequent disbandment. An unpublished study undertaken for the Subcommittee by the Congressional Budget Office in June 1982 arrived at more balanced conclusions. Although its appraisal was not markedly different from that of the Department of Defense – in that it estimated the cost of relocation and possible prepositioning of equipment as much greater than the annual recurring savings that would result from a smaller presence in Europe – it also acknowledged that substantial savings would be made if troop withdrawals from Europe resulted in a smaller army.[15] Unless, therefore, forces pulled back from Europe were demobilized, the financial savings would be slight at best. Nevertheless, the proposals for reductions in the number of American troops deployed in Europe are once again on the agenda. Yet this idea is only one of several strands in the current debate, the main elements of which are identified in the next chapter.

4 The pressures for change

In June 1984, the congressional pressure for American troop withdrawals from Western Europe reached, albeit very briefly, a level of intensity not seen since the debates of 1971 and 1973. The proceedings had a strong sense of *déjà vu* as the administration lobbied vigorously to head off a troop withdrawal amendment that otherwise might well have passed the Senate. For all the parallels with the debates on the Mansfield Amendments of the early 1970s, there was one important difference: the author of the Amendment was Sam Nunn who, as a freshman senator, had been one of the leading figures in the fight against the Mansfield Amendment of 1974. In fact it was the 1974 debate which had established Nunn's reputation as one of the leading authorities in the Senate on security and defence issues – a reputation which he subsequently consolidated by producing several influential reports on NATO's strategy and force levels, in which he highlighted the need for the Alliance to augment its conventional forces.

That it was Nunn who was now introducing legislation which could result in a reduction of US troops in Europe may have had a certain irony, but it also meant that the administration and the European allies had to take the proposal seriously. In the previous two years, Senator Ted Stevens of Alaska, Chairman of the Defense Appropriations Subcommittee and Republican Whip, had taken the lead in focusing attention on the issue. Whereas Stevens was, in large part, adopting a punitive stance based on his distaste for European policies towards the Polish crisis and the Siberian gas pipeline, Nunn was opting for a more constructive approach by explicitly linking the continued deployment of the existing level of troops to greater defence efforts by the Europeans. Yet

29

Nunn was also expressing the general sense of dissatisfaction with what was widely regarded as the European failure to shoulder an equitable share of the defence burden. His amendment appealed to senators who resented the stark contrast between American defence spending — which had increased markedly in the late 1970s and early 1980s — and European spending, which had gone up far more gradually and in some cases actually declined in real terms. Although the Nunn Amendment can be understood partly as a tactical ploy in the perennial Alliance bargaining over burden-sharing, it was not motivated solely by considerations of equity. Nunn was attempting to force the Europeans to take specific measures which would increase NATO's prospects for sustained conventional defence. As he pointed out, it was pointless for the United States to have ammunition stocks for 30 days if the allies would run out of ammunition much sooner: 'If we do not have allies that are going to do their part, there is no need for the American taxpayer to spend billions and billions and billions of dollars. We can have a tripwire for a lot less.'[1]

This concern with military effectiveness was evident in the terms of Nunn's proposal. The troop withdrawals were to take place on a phased basis of 30,000 a year over three years, beginning in 1987. Yet Nunn also offered an incentive plan whereby this could be avoided. If the Europeans actually met their commitment to increase defence budgets by 3 per cent; or brought up their levels of ammunition to a point at which they could keep their forces supplied for thirty days of combat; or took steps to protect those aircraft from the United States which would be deployed to Europe as part of America's reinforcement capability, then the withdrawals would not take place.

Even with these options, the Amendment was rejected by 55 votes to 41 as too drastic. Nevertheless, a compromise measure introduced by Senator Cohen of Maine, and passed overwhelmingly by 94 votes to 3, threatened to freeze US troop levels in Europe unless the Secretary of Defense was able to certify that the allies had made significant progress in meeting the goals established by Nunn.

In spite of its defeat, therefore, the Nunn Amendment may portend a greater willingness on the part of many legislators to contemplate some reductions in the American military contingent in Western Europe. Had it not been for party discipline and some intense lobbying by the administration, the Amendment could well have received a majority in its favour. Furthermore, it is significant that although Nunn is a committed Atlanticist attempting to prod the allies into adopting what he regards as a more effective military posture, troop-cut proposals of the kind he introduced appeal to those who are far less well-disposed towards the Alliance. It seems likely that proposals for troop withdrawals will continue to surface in the years ahead, and it is conceivable that they will win widespread support. There are powerful forces in American politics and society militating against Western Europe's retaining the priority in American military planning that it has had for 35 years. Consequently, the Europeans would do well to ponder the possibility that at some future date there will be a far smaller American contingent on the Continent than there is at the moment. Explicitly considering this prospect, therefore, could have considerable utility as an exercise in contingency planning.

It is, of course, possible to exaggerate the pressure for troop withdrawals. After all, the most salient feature of congressional demands for cuts in the American presence in Europe is that so far they have not been successful. Nevertheless, it is worth emphasizing that there is no domestic political constituency with a vested interest in their retention. Furthermore, the concern over the American budget deficit and the difficulties of reducing it while simultaneously increasing defence expenditure will make it necessary to establish a clearer set of priorities and to make savings wherever possible.

Against this background there could well be a growing sentiment that Western Europe has had more than its fair share of support from the United States, and that in the future far more attention needs to be devoted to other areas in which the threat from the Soviet Union is more immediate and the ability of other states to act as a counter is far more limited. The fact that the United States, in preparing for possible involvement in South-West Asia, sees itself as protecting the interests of Western Europe and Japan as much as its own welfare strengthens this tendency. It also adds to the arguments of those in the Congress and the Executive branch who believe that the emphasis on coalition defence with transatlantic and transpacific allies, which has been the main theme of American security policy throughout the postwar period, needs to be reduced or even abandoned. They would prefer to see a strategy based on 'maritime supremacy': a 600-ship navy, and forces which are highly mobile and capable not only of rapid deployment to cope with emergent threats, but of equally rapid withdrawal in their aftermath.[2] Ground defences and permanent land-based deployments are, in this view, regarded as undesirable strategically and as a wasteful diversion of resources from roles and missions necessary to contain what has become a global threat from the Soviet Union.

In many respects this attitude harks back to some of the ideas proposed by Herbert Hoover and Senator Robert Taft during the Great Debate of 1951. Although the 'maritime supremacy' strategy goes well beyond the Fortress America concept advocated by Hoover and Taft, it reiterates the emphasis on control of the seas found in their prescriptions, and shares the same antipathy to the notion of substantial ground forces permanently deployed on the Eurasian land mass. Such an approach appears particularly attractive during a period of suspicion and disillusionment with allies, but the unilateralist strand which it reflects is a long-standing feature of American foreign policy and is unlikely to be weakened to any notable extent by improvements in Alliance relations.

In other words, the pressures for change in America's military posture overseas seem unlikely to diminish and may well increase through the 1980s. And whereas in the past there were always committed Atlanticists who were prepared to do battle on behalf of the Europeans, this group is unlikely to have the same kind of influence in the future as it did in the past. The days when the old guard of diplomatic and military officials could come out of retirement to help defeat a Mansfield-type amendment are over. Furthermore, as the Nunn Amendment demonstrated, some of the remaining Atlanticists are themselves becoming disillusioned with the allies. Others have adopted a global perspective. An example of the changing perspectives can be found in an address in March 1984 by the then Under-Secretary of State for Political Affairs, Lawrence Eagleburger, traditionally one of the staunchest defenders of the US commitment to Europe.

The main theme of Eagleburger's statement was that although the Atlantic Alliance remained vital to the United States, 'global foreign policy imperatives' would increasingly demand American attention, time and imagination.[3] Furthermore, he identified the growing tendency in American foreign policy to look to the Pacific rather than the Atlantic as one of the most dynamic regions of economic growth. As he noted, 'it is little remarked, but nonetheless a remarkable fact that since 1978 we have traded more with the Pacific basin than with Europe: in 1982 the difference amounted to $13,000 million. The American and Japanese economies account for about one third of the world's total gross national product. Last year, Japan was the second largest buyer of America's products (after Canada) – and yet only one of several increasingly important Asian trading partners.'[4]

The implications of this may be all the more significant because of internal changes in the United States itself. The centre of economic power has moved from the North-East and the Atlantic seaboard to the sunbelt of the South and West. Not only is the Southern Rim, as it is sometimes called, the most dynamic part of the American economy, but it is also the one which looks to the burgeoning economies of the Pacific rather than to Europe for trading links.

This trend away from Atlanticism is likely to be intensified by long-term, demographic changes. The growing number of Americans with Asian roots will encourage a preoccupation with the Pacific, while the emergence of the Hispanics as perhaps the leading ethnic group in the United States will almost certainly require that greater attention be given to the needs of Central and South America. Indeed, the growing preoccupation with Central America has been a major theme in the policies of the Reagan Administration. The Kissinger Commission, which reported in January 1984, was unequivocal in its conclusion that the region was vital to the security of the United States and should be given the same priority as commitments in Europe, Asia and the Persian Gulf.[5] Although US military involvement in the area is held in check by analogies with Vietnam, which, whatever their accuracy, have a powerful emotional impact, it is not clear that these will be sufficient to prohibit direct military intervention. The long-term consequence, therefore, could be a widening of the gap between commitments and capabilities. Even the Reagan Administration's increased spending on defence is unlikely to be sufficient to overcome this, especially in view of the importance it attaches to the Gulf. Consequently, the primacy that Europe has long enjoyed in American foreign policy seems likely to diminish.

This does not mean that the United States will become indifferent to its European allies. The very proximity of Western Europe to the Soviet Union makes this virtually impossible. What it does imply is that demands for greater burden-sharing will become even more intense. The same demands, together with those for reductions in the American troop contingent in Europe, were at their height during the period of American involvement in Vietnam. US military entanglements outside Europe in the future would almost certainly have a similar impact. Whether they would actually require reductions in the forces deployed in Europe is not certain, but a large-scale intervention in Central America or the use of the Rapid Deployment Force in the Gulf would almost certainly undermine American ability to reinforce its European garrison should a crisis simultaneously occur in Europe. The implication is that American demands for both compensation in Europe and direct European participation in out-of-area contingencies are likely to intensify rather than abate.

The other difficulty with American involvement elsewhere is that it seems likely to put additional strains on an Atlantic agenda that is already overloaded with problems. Should the Europeans not provide the military or diplomatic support the United States expects, then demands for troop reductions could well become more strident. This is all the more probable because of the existing dissatisfaction with European defence efforts and the disappointment over what is seen as an unwillingness on the part of many Europeans to share burdens and make sacrifices for their own security.

In short, the pressures for a far-reaching reappraisal of the American military presence in Western Europe may be irreversible, although the outcome of such a review would not inevitably be a draw-down in the American contingent. As well as the pressures for reduction, there are pressures for reform and, indeed, for strengthening the American presence as part of an attempt to reduce NATO's dependence on nuclear weapons. It is widely felt that Soviet advances at the nuclear level have made it much more difficult for the United States to rely on threats of nuclear escalation to compensate for conventional weakness. Ironically, one of the leading proponents of this position is Sam Nunn, who has argued that 'Soviet essential equivalence in the nuclear balance must be met by NATO essential equivalence in the conventional balance'.[6] Similarly, the proposals for a 'no first use' declaration by NATO are predicated on the assumption that the Alliance is able to enhance its conventional capabilities and move from a posture of deterrence through nuclear retaliation to one of deterrence through denial, in which the emphasis is on preventing Warsaw Pact territorial gains rather than inflicting costs on the Soviet homeland. And in this connection a reduction of US conventional forces would be inopportune to say the least.

An additional consideration is that there have been considerable improvements in Warsaw Pact conventional forces over the last decade or so, and it would appear somewhat imprudent for the United States to opt out of its traditional policy of attempting to offset Soviet advances by improvements in its own capabilities. Furthermore, the assessments that have been made about Soviet doctrine and strategy acknowledge the emphasis that is placed on strategic surprise and concentration of effort in order to provide the rapid breakthrough and exploitation necessary for a short decisive campaign. As one analyst has put it: 'Calls for continuous operations and high rates of advance indicate that Moscow favours a speedy resolution of any conflict, before NATO's superior resources could be brought to bear, or before the West could reach a decision to use nuclear weapons. Warsaw Pact armies have forgone the support units thought necessary for prolonged operations and thus can field more combat units and more combat power than Western armies, given the same level of manpower and equipment.'[7] Although NATO at the moment obviously depends very heavily on mobilization of reserves and on reinforcements from the United States, and will continue to do so, this assessment of Soviet strategy and capabilities underlines the importance of forces being in position on the Central Front. From this perspective the United States should not be considering withdrawing forces from Europe, but rather the various ways in which these forces could be made more efficient and effective. There has already been considerable debate about the ways in which this might be done, and some of the proposals are considered in the next chapter.

5 Strengthening NATO's conventional forces

One of the consequences of NATO's decision of December 1979 to modernize its long-range theatre nuclear forces was that it focused unprecedented public attention on the role of nuclear weapons in NATO strategy. The deployment of cruise missiles and Pershing IIs seemed to many critics to symbolize the excessive dependence of the Alliance on nuclear weapons. When, therefore, four former high-ranking American officials – McGeorge Bundy, George Kennan, Robert McNamara and Gerard Smith – proposed that NATO adopt a posture founded on the principle of 'no first use' of nuclear weapons, their arguments received widespread, if not always uncritical, attention.[1] And although the 'no first use' proposal itself has been dismissed by many European and American officials as going too far, it has helped to arouse considerable interest in the strengthening of conventional forces. Even German analysts, who have traditionally strongly resisted any idea of fighting a sustained and large-scale conventional war on German territory, accepted that there might be considerable merit in a NATO move towards a position of 'delayed first use'.[2] It has also been suggested that this would help to close the gap between deterrence and reassurance which has opened up as Western Europe has increasingly relied on American nuclear weapons for its security.[3] The movement in this direction has been given further impetus by the fact that a number of peace groups have attempted to go beyond pacifist demands for unilateral disarmament and consider practical ways in which NATO might reduce its reliance on nuclear weapons. As a result, it has been suggested that it might be possible to re-establish a defence consensus in Western Europe around the idea of stronger conventional forces.

Proposals for strengthening NATO's conventional forces are far from new. Analysts such as Steven Canby have long been arguing that a more imaginative approach to conventional defence in Europe would enable NATO to make far better use of its available resources.[4] In the early 1980s, however, the upsurge of interest in such ideas has generated a large number of recommendations extending from schemes for 'non-provocative defence'[5] to plans for exploiting existing and emerging technologies to implement roles and missions which have hitherto relied on nuclear weapons. Furthermore, General Rogers has argued that with an annual 4 per cent real increase in defence budgets NATO would be much better able to defend itself against a Warsaw Pact attack and would not have to resort to the premature use of nuclear weapons.

The problem with many of these ideas is that they focus rather narrowly on military concerns and pay insufficient attention to political and economic constraints both at the Alliance level and at the level of individual nations. There are several criteria against which any suggestions for reforming NATO's military posture must be assessed.[6] As well as meeting the obvious standard of enhancing deterrence and defence, a reformed strategy should also increase the prospects for crisis management, be compatible with measures of détente, provide a basis for political consensus within the Alliance, and be affordable within the existing constraints on resources and manpower. The problem with these requirements is that they are not necessarily compatible. Measures which strengthen NATO's capacity for a sustained conventional defence, for example, might pose problems of consensus as well as impose a strain on available resources. Some would also argue that a capacity for sustained conventional defence is not necessarily synonymous with an enhancement of deterrence. Similarly, proposals designed to strengthen deterrence might have undesirable implications for arms control. Furthermore, not all governments will attach the same value to each of these criteria. The Europeans concerned about maintaining détente may be less inclined than Washington to embrace improvements which could appear provocative to the Soviet Union and which might jeopardize crisis management. With this in mind, it is necessary to consider several of the more important variations on the theme of strengthening NATO's conventional capabilities.

Perhaps one of the most important ideas to have emerged in the recent debate over NATO's force posture is that increasing reliance should be placed on new and emerging technologies which provide a capacity for target acquisition and precision guidance at far greater distances than has hitherto been contemplated. Enhanced surveillance techniques, improved capabilities for command, control, communications and intelligence (C^3I), and a new generation of sophisticated munitions and submunitions appear to offer the Alliance options that have hitherto been available only through the use of nuclear weapons. Their proponents also argue that they are sufficiently effective to restore the flexibility of flexible response, and to do so at reasonable cost. NATO could get itself off the 'nuclear hook' by investing in new weapons which would be used to hit Soviet and East European airfields and other military targets deep behind the battle area.[7] These weapons would be capable of destroying Soviet second-echelon forces before they could reinforce the first echelon and thereby facilitate or exploit any breakthrough in NATO's defences. Such reliance on high technology, in which NATO nations have a considerable advantage over the Soviet Union, is seen as a natural way of offsetting the Warsaw Pact's superiority in manpower and tanks.

The impetus for moving in this direction has come from several different sources: the US Army, with its concepts of AirLand Battle and AirLand 2000; General Rogers and SHAPE, with their ideas for Follow-On Force Attack; and the US Defense Department's Office of Research and Engineering. The proposals differ considerably in terms of targets and of the depth behind the Forward Edge of the Battle Area (FEBA) at which the strikes would take place. The AirLand Battle concept encompasses attacks up to 150 kilometres beyond the FEBA, whereas the ideas coming from SHAPE contemplate targets at a distance of 300 kilometres.[8] The notion of deep strikes, of course, is not new. NATO has long had plans to hit airfields and other military targets in Eastern Europe. The emerging technologies (ET), however, are believed to offer a means of doing this more efficiently, more effectively and less dangerously than in the past.

Further support for ET has come from prominent defence analysts concerned about the declining credibility of flexible response as currently constituted. Yet there are several reasons for suggesting that such an approach needs to be treated with caution. NATO has traditionally embraced technology, albeit primarily nuclear technology, as a way of providing defence and deterrence on the cheap, and once again appears to be 'groping for technical panaceas',[9] although this time at the conventional rather than the nuclear level. There are a number of unanswered questions, regarding the new technologies and tactics, which provoke both scepticism and concern. NATO cannot afford to ignore opportunities for strengthening its defensive capability by greater use of technology and more imaginative tactics, but if ET is evaluated against the criteria set out above, its advantages are not nearly so clear-cut as is sometimes suggested.

In the first place, it is necessary to distinguish between those possibilities which are likely to be available by 1990 and which can be costed with reasonable certainty, and those which are rather more remote and for which even approximate cost estimates are virtually meaningless. For example, the possibility of using missiles with non-nuclear warheads against airfields would fall into the first category of capabilities, which NATO could realistically expect to obtain. In contrast, the ability to hit highly mobile targets at great distances seems likely to remain far more elusive and may not actually be attainable by the year 2000.

Even if the technology is readily available, it is not certain that it will have the impact that some of the more extravagant claims suggest. The value of hitting second-echelon forces, in particular, may be less than is sometimes assumed. In the event of a war in Europe – which many analysts believe the Soviet Union would do its utmost to avoid – Warsaw Pact forces would aim to achieve surprise and thereby penetrate NATO's defences with divisional-size forces. For the Warsaw Pact the first wave may be the most important one, and would aim to disrupt and destroy NATO's nuclear capabilities, its C^3I facilities, and its reinforcement capacity. Striking second-echelon forces, therefore, may not have an immediate impact in slowing down the Pact advance. Indeed, some analysts argue not only that it is the first echelon which poses the greatest danger, but that the focus on deep strikes might actually divert resources and attention away from what should be the main priority: forward defence against the initial wave. This is not to suggest that ET is of no value; merely that some of the targeting priorities which have been discussed require re-examination. Shallow strikes rather than deep strikes may be the key to maximizing the defensive capability available to the Alliance in the future.

The extent to which ET weapons bolster deterrence is bound up with the more fundamental question of whether strengthening conventional forces adds to deterrence by increasing credibility, or detracts from it by encouraging the Soviet Union to believe that a conventional war in Europe is possible without escalation to nuclear weapons. Although refurbishing NATO's conventional forces no longer seems to be regarded as incompatible with the nuclear component of deterrence (a belief that was prevalent in the 1960s), there is still a reluctance on the part of some Europeans to go too far in this direction. Indeed, there has always been a certain ambivalence about the rationale for stronger conventional forces: on the one hand they provide non-nuclear options and thereby hold out the prospect that a war in Europe could be kept limited; on the other it is suggested that the use of nuclear weapons becomes credible only in the context of a large-scale conventional war. In this connection, the impact of ET may be far less straightforward than is sometimes assumed.

Although ET has been presented as a fairly safe option which offers a way of avoiding the nuclear dilemmas that have long bedevilled NATO, there are grounds for supposing that the use of some of the new weapon systems being discussed would have an immediate escalatory effect. Deep strikes, for example, using a new generation of conventional missiles, could pressure the Soviet Union into launching a nuclear strike of its own. In the confusion of battle, Soviet leaders may be unwilling or unable to differentiate clearly between the use of conventional and nuclear systems by the Alliance. At the very least, Moscow would require a very sophisticated capacity for warning and damage assessment. If, therefore, NATO deploys conventionally armed cruise or ballistic missiles which are not readily distinguishable from their nuclear counterparts, the results may be rather different from those intended.

An additional twist is added to this problem by the fact that any conventional war in Europe (even one in which these systems were not available) would create considerable anxieties for Moscow about the survivability of its strategic forces. Barry Posen has argued very convincingly that intense conventional hostilities in Europe could be perceived by the Soviet leadership as camouflage for a pre-emptive NATO strike against their strategic nuclear forces, thereby encouraging the Soviet Union to go first.[10] And in circumstances in which conventional missiles were being used to strike targets deep in Eastern Europe and conceivably the western part of the Soviet Union, these concerns would be intensified. In other words, although ET systems may raise the nuclear threshold in the sense that NATO would not have to resort to an early and deliberate use of nuclear weapons in response to conventional attack, they could lower the threshold for Moscow.

This is not to suggest that NATO should refrain from exploiting emerging technologies, but that full consideration should be given to how they will affect the ability of the two sides to manage a crisis or limit hostilities. Part of the problem here is that the term 'raising the nuclear threshold' is imprecise. It has come to mean primarily the postponement of the time when NATO is faced with a choice between military defeat and resort to the use of nuclear weapons. Yet this is only one dimension of the problem and one which ignores the initial idea of what a threshold entailed.

Perhaps the most important and desirable characteristic of a threshold or firebreak is clarity. Crossing it implies a qualitative change in the situation or a marked discontinuity with preceding events. A threshold is far stronger when it is qualitative in nature and based on prominent distinctions, or on what Thomas Schelling described as 'saliency'.[11] The problem with some of the new technologies and tactics is that they threaten to blur the distinction between conventional and nuclear hostilities. If the aim is to make any use of nuclear weapons (as opposed simply to NATO first use) less likely, ET may not be an unmixed blessing. While the conventional/nuclear dilemmas facing NATO would be eased, those facing the Warsaw Pact would be intensified. The question arises whether this is desirable or not. If it is, there is a rather ironic implication: although ET might strengthen deterrence, this would be achieved because it adds to the likelihood of escalation rather than to the sustainability of conventional defence. To the extent that deterrence in Europe is based ultimately on the possibility of events getting out of control, ET may add to deterrence. The irony is that it has been presented as something which will minimize the escalatory potential of hostilities.

If emerging technologies and new tactics strengthen deterrence – albeit not in ways originally intended – they could at the same time jeopardize crisis management and undermine attempts to limit hostilities. The qualities which make ET an additional deterrent pose problems as soon as other criteria are brought in. Not only would the use of conventionally armed cruise and ballistic missiles, for example, make it more difficult to maintain control over events and bring hostilities in Europe to a close, but the extensive deployment of such systems could increase the pressures on the Soviet Union to initiate hostilities with a pre-emptive nuclear strike. 'Use them or lose them' dilemmas are not confined to NATO. This is not to suggest that all the new technologies are equally dangerous; NATO has to distinguish between them and decide which of the competing criteria are most important. As Manfred Wörner, the German Defence Minister, has stated, the Alliance requires a 'conceptual framework' within which the benefits and drawbacks can be explicitly and systematically assessed.[12]

The problem is that different members of the Alliance might have very different views about the importance to be attached to particular criteria. If it is not handled with great care, ET could pose serious problems for Alliance consensus and cohesion. The Federal Republic in particular has two main difficulties with ET, especially in the deep-strike role. The first is that, for Bonn, there is no substitute for forward defence, and anything which threatens to divert attention and resources away from that — especially in a period of constrained budgets and manpower — is unwelcome. The second is that the West German government, understandably, feels ambivalent about new weapon systems and tactics which appear to transform NATO from a strictly defensive alliance into a more offensively oriented organization. Bonn is still concerned with the maintenance of détente in Europe, and would be sensitive to weapon systems which further jeopardize it, especially in view of the controversy over the modernization of long-range theatre nuclear forces.

There is also the problem of costs. Although the new technologies offer cheaper ways of implementing certain roles and missions, and therefore might theoretically result in lower expenditures, in some cases they will almost certainly run up against bureaucratic inertia and a concern with maintaining traditional capabilities. As a result, they may be regarded less as a replacement for existing weapon systems than as an adjunct to them, and many of the hoped-for savings could prove difficult to realize. Furthermore, although some of the weapon systems might prove relatively cheap, the improvements in C^3I facilities required to exploit them to the full could prove much more expensive. Consequently, in spite of their having been widely heralded as a cheap and effective way of reducing NATO's dependence on nuclear weapons, emerging technologies may not be as cheap or as effective as is sometimes claimed. And, as already suggested, their effect on the nuclear threshold is likely to be far more ambiguous than is generally acknowledged. In terms of the criteria established above, therefore, the advantages they offer are far from unequivocal.

Much the same is true of a second proposal which has recently been made: that NATO should adopt a posture based on a retaliatory offensive into Eastern Europe.[13] This suggestion, by Samuel Huntington, rests upon the argument that deterrence through denial is less effective than deterrence through threats to inflict high costs upon the adversary. In Huntington's view, conventional deterrence is no substitute for nuclear deterrence unless it also contains a retaliatory ingredient directed against things the adversary values very highly. Planning for a retaliatory offensive against Eastern Europe would achieve this. It would also 'capitalize on the uncertainties and fears that the Soviets have concerning the reliability of their East European allies, and the uncertainties and fears that the governments of these countries have concerning the reliability of their own peoples. It would put at potential risk the system of controls over Eastern Europe that the Soviets have developed over thirty years and which they consider critical to their own security.'[14] Another advantage of such an approach is that it would make efficient use of American forces in the south of Germany. Although these forces are in the wrong place to counter a Pact offensive across the north German plain, they are ideally suited for a retaliatory strike into Eastern Europe. Furthermore, Huntington argues, the strategy would be compatible with the AirLand Battle doctrine with its emphasis on manoeuvre and deep strike, and would merely bring flexible response up to date in the new circumstances of the 1980s.

Against all this, however, it can be argued that the strategy suffers from several defects: when examined against the criteria set out above, it scores very highly on some but very badly on others. Although in terms of deterrence and defence Huntington makes a very persuasive case, this is probably offset by the impact of such a change on the prospects for crisis management. Deterrence is a major element in the peaceful resolution of crises, but there is a narrow line between this and a posture which provokes the adversary into pre-emptive action. If NATO explicitly espoused the idea of a retaliatory offensive into Eastern Europe, it could make crises much less manageable. Not only would the stakes for the Soviet Union be greatly increased, but the distinction between retaliatory action and aggressive action would also be blurred. What makes this all the more disquieting is that reassurance could be as important as deterrence in any crisis in Eastern Europe; and an offensive strategy by NATO would not provide it.

Soviet military intervention to maintain order and stability in its bloc has been a central if unpalatable feature of the postwar international order, and the acquiescence of the West in Soviet actions has ensured that the crises have been localized. In circumstances in which the Soviet Union was considering whether to intervene but knew that NATO had a strategy for an offensive into Eastern Europe, the requirement to take precautions against this would be overwhelming. If precautionary moves by Warsaw Pact forces were then interpreted by NATO as preparations for a move into Western Europe, NATO forces, too, would be placed on a high level of alert. This in turn would exacerbate Soviet security concerns. Although the resulting tension might still be defused, a change in NATO strategy along the lines advocated by Huntington could transform Soviet bloc crises into East–West crises, with dangerous and unpredictable consequences.

An additional problem would be its effect on East–West relations in Europe even without continuing instability in the Soviet bloc. The détente of the 1970s was predicated on an explicit acceptance by the West of the *status quo* in Eastern Europe. The Helsinki Final Act of 1975, in particular, was of enormous significance to the Soviet Union, since it gave a degree of legitimacy to the Soviet position that had hitherto been lacking. The strategy of a retaliatory offensive, although not intended to challenge this, would perhaps be seen in this way by the Soviet leaders. Coming after the deployment of cruise missiles and Pershing IIs, a reform in NATO strategy along the lines advocated by Huntington would merely intensify Soviet paranoia and further undermine the residual détente in Europe. It is partly because of such concerns that the strategy is unlikely to receive the endorsement of many Europeans. Although it might have support among some segments of the

European military, it would be a matter of extreme political sensitivity, and would therefore be unlikely to generate much enthusiasm at the governmental, parliamentary or public level. In the European public debate of the early 1980s, it is ideas of non-provocative defence which have attracted attention. Retaliatory offensives would be presented by European critics and by the Soviet Union as anything but non-provocative.

In this connection, there are crucial questions about the extent to which the Western Alliance should be sensitive to Soviet fears about their own security. It is sometimes difficult to distinguish between real paranoia on the part of the Soviet Union and paranoia which is contrived in an effort to undermine the willingness of the West to go ahead with measures designed to offset Soviet military predominance. Where it is genuine, there must be doubts about whether the West can do anything to manage or reduce it. Furthermore, a policy in which the desire to be non-provocative is paramount would give the Soviet Union a *de facto* veto over NATO's force-planning decisions. At the very least, incorporating these considerations into planning could be self-defeating. Creating a defence system that would be less effective than it might be is not the most appropriate way of dealing with an adversary who appears oblivious to these broader considerations and intent on creating a system capable of applying maximum force as efficiently as possible. There is also a danger that West European insistence on integrating some of these ideas into NATO's posture could further alienate the United States, which would tend to interpret a concern with 'non-provocation' as further evidence of allied weakness. Accusations that Western Europe had been Finlandized would almost inevitably follow.

Serious though these dangers are, they should not be regarded as prohibitive. To argue that consideration should be given to notions of crisis management and the avoidance of provocation is not to imply that the Soviet Union should be allowed to determine NATO force levels or tactics. It is simply to suggest that military strength *per se* is only one component of security in Europe. Nor should the fact that the Soviet Union does not appear to be concerned about crisis management mean that NATO can afford to be indifferent to it. To recognize that NATO has considerable self-interest in managing or preventing crises in Europe — regardless of whether the Soviet Union acknowledges that this is a matter of mutual interest — is not to indulge in appeasement. Non-provocation and stability are not intended to be a substitute for deterrence and defence, but a supplement to these more traditional but ultimately incomplete means of enhancing security.

If one danger is that European concern with these broader considerations will alienate the United States, another is that Washington will push reluctant Europeans in directions in which they would prefer not to go. One of the problems with Huntington's recommendations is that he seems oblivious to this. Although he recognizes that, after the United States, the other key locus of decision-making is the Federal Republic, he sees no reason why Bonn should not find it an attractive option: 'One would think that German leaders would endorse a military strategy that, in comparison to the alternatives, promised to produce stronger deterrence at lower cost, to reduce the probability that nuclear weapons would be used in the territory of the Federal Republic, and to shift at least some of the fighting, if war did occur, from the Federal Republic to East Germany and Czechoslovakia. It is hard to see why it might be good politics in West Germany to oppose such a move.'[15] Huntington's argument, however, appears to be almost one-dimensional and to treat security in Europe as dependent only on NATO's military preparations. As soon as it is accepted that there are other criteria which may be relevant to such a proposal, it is hard to see why the Federal Republic would not oppose the idea of retaliatory offensives.

It is understandable, though, that many American analysts and officials become rather impatient with the Federal Republic. There is a sense in which West German political sensitivities render it difficult for the Alliance to take initiatives which depart to any great extent from the notion of forward defence, even though, as William Mako has pointed out, forward defence carries with it 'the risk of penetration and encirclement'.[16] Defence in depth and the possibility of trading space for time are excluded by German political anxieties. So too are strategies which have an offensive character.

The Federal Republic has also been reluctant to contemplate the creation of fixed defences along the intra-German border, partly because this would appear to give further legitimacy to the division of the nation, but also because of protests from local farmers. Yet measures of this kind would almost certainly have considerable utility. As one analyst has observed, 'it is an almost bizarre hiatus in the NATO defence system that no fortifications have been constructed on its fronts'.[17] The fullest proposal for such measures is one by John Tillson, who has suggested that NATO spend around $3 billion over several years on special landscaping to create obstacles specifically designed to prevent a rapid tank breakthrough. The creation of ditches, minefields, and concrete obstacles would be relatively inexpensive, yet would help to slow the rate of any Pact advance. This terrain modification could be supplemented by 'prepared emplacements for use by tanks and artillery, as well as observation posts for calling and controlling the use of long-range artillery, anti-tank clusters, or remotely controlled precision-guided munitions. Such fortifications could also include numerous small concrete bunkers to provide shelter and support for light infantry forces.'[18]

There are several advantages to a system of this kind. It would have a clearly defensive orientation and, unlike the two previous proposals, would not in any way provoke the Soviet Union. And, by giving NATO extra time in which to mobilize its forces, it would make it much more difficult for the Pact forces to launch an effective surprise attack. Indeed, as R. K. Betts has pointed out, there is a sense in which these two arguments are mutually reinforcing. 'A fortified line could soften political obstacles to minimizing the impact of surprise. If NATO units are permitted to move out of garrisons, say, only 12 hours before Soviet tanks come over the border, they will be more effective than they would without prefortification. Political disincentives to authorize movement forward should also be less. Fewer men and tanks would have to sprint toward the border, and this makes the change in posture less arguably threatening to the East.'[19] Such a change would also give NATO forces a greater degree of flexibility in responding to Soviet attacks. The initial defensive positions could be manned by a mix of regular forces and light Territorial Army reservists. This would free the regular mechanized forces to act as a mobile reserve capable of responding rapidly to any breaches in the front resulting from a successful concentration of Warsaw Pact forces. Without a large operational reserve, the defences would do no more than delay a Pact advance; with such a reserve it could help to deny Pact forces a quick victory and give NATO a formidable capability for a counter-offensive to regain lost territory.

One thing on which most analysts of Soviet military policy and doctrine agree is that Moscow would aim for a rapid and decisive victory before nuclear weapons come into play. Preparations which make this less feasible could add significantly to deterrence in Europe. At the same time, the approach advocated by Tillson and Betts would strengthen rather than undermine the prospects for managing crises in Europe. However, quite apart from the political difficulties it might arouse in the Federal Republic, such a proposal suffers from deeply ingrained prejudices against fixed defences. Furthermore, given the limited resources available, it might be that the money could be allocated to more important priorities. Field commanders, for example, would probably prefer capabilities such as air cavalry which would enhance mobility. But despite the opportunity cost argument, it may be that some combination of static defence positions and mobile operational reserves provides the optimum posture. This kind of proposal might also go some way towards reconciling forward defence and defence in depth. Prepared defensive positions near the border could form part of a defence in depth based upon the natural barriers provided by cities. Here again, units of the German Territorial Army could make an important contribution. As has been argued, German territorial formations would be particularly useful in defending urban areas.[20] The defensive potential of what Paul Bracken termed 'urban sprawl' could thereby be exploited to provide a series of 'hedgehogs' which would delay and channel advancing Pact forces.[21] 'In effect, the cities and towns of the German countryside would be transformed after mobilization into a checkerboard of strongpoints around which NATO's own mechanized formations could manoeuvre to seal off any Soviet penetration.'[22]

The virtues of such a strategy are considerable. Not only would it fulfil the political imperative of forward defence, but it would also accommodate the military requirement of defence in depth. In addition, it would combine elements of attrition and manoeuvre. It would minimize the risks of surprise attack and make clear to the Soviet Union that it could not expect a quick and easy victory. At the same time, the emphasis on defence would be compatible with continued détente in Europe, and it would not demand a great deal in the way of additional resources. The main requirement would be that NATO make better use of its existing capabilities, rather than rely upon substantial increases in the defence budgets of its member states.

Despite these advantages, there are two major question marks over reliance on a defensive strategy of this kind. The first concerns the disparity in conventional forces between NATO and the Warsaw Pact in Central Europe. The second concerns the role of nuclear weapons in NATO strategy. Each of these must now be examined.

Although some would claim that Warsaw Pact superiority makes planning to halt, let alone defeat, a massive attack unrealistic, the conventional military balance in Central Europe is sufficiently complex — even without major improvements in NATO's force structure — to make the Soviet Union doubt that it would win easily or quickly. Even on an optimistic analysis by Moscow, the imponderables outweigh the certainties. And if the Soviet Union engages in the same kind of 'worst case thinking' that is often apparent in the West, it would see so much which could go wrong. The reliability of East European armies, for example, is not something which can be taken for granted, especially if hostilities in Central Europe become protracted. Indeed, concern over instability in the Soviet bloc could act as an additional inhibition on Soviet leaders contemplating a move against Western Europe. Furthermore, the Soviet Union has to contend with a hostile China on its disputed eastern border, and would be reluctant to become too embroiled in the west for fear of offering Peking an opportunity to provoke trouble elsewhere. In addition to these broad political factors, there are military considerations which induce a high degree of caution. Although the attacker has the initiative in the time and place of his assault, there are sufficient questions regarding the necessary ratio of offensive to defensive forces, the impact of new precision-guided munitions, and the possible use of nuclear weapons to ensure that a war in Europe is regarded as a hazardous undertaking with an outcome for the Soviet Union which, at best, is inherently uncertain and, at worst, disastrous. In other words, even without a programme for strengthening NATO's defences along the lines suggested above, the result of Soviet aggression in Europe is far from a foregone conclusion.

Much, of course, would depend on whether either or both sides had reinforced their conventional forces. Although assessments differ regarding the possibility of a sudden attack from a standing start by the Warsaw Pact, it seems likely that the Soviet leadership would consider this to be a very high risk option. Furthermore, it is difficult to envisage a situation in Europe in which the Soviets decided to launch an un-provoked surprise attack. The Soviet Union would have no incentive for doing this, especially in view of the benefits it derives from East–West trade. And if there were a crisis in Europe in which both sides were in a state of high alert, then the Soviet Union could not rely on surprise. If the bolt from the blue is unrealistic, the alternative of a reinforced attack might not look attractive either.

Nevertheless, a situation in which mobilization had begun could be highly dangerous for NATO. Part of the problem for the Alliance is that it relies so heavily on reinforcements from the continental United States. In the midst of a worsening crisis in Central Europe, there would almost inevitably be division both within and between member govern-ments about the need for reinforcement and the appropriate time at which national forces earmarked and assigned to SACEUR should actually come under his control. The main divisions would probably be between those who felt that reinforcements from across the Atlantic could inflame the crisis and exacerbate tensions and those who believed that without such demonstrations of resolve the Soviet Union might begin to doubt NATO's credibility.

The key issue in these circumstances is to decide whether it is more important to avoid taking steps which could result in the crisis getting out of hand, or to convince the adversary that he cannot achieve a *fait accompli*. If it is the first, there would be considerable incentive not to deploy reinforcements for fear of provoking a Soviet attack; if it is the second, the main concern would be to restore deterrence. This would require tangible evidence of American will and resolve, evidence that could best be provided by the large-scale and rapid deployment of US forces from the continental United States to supplement those already deployed in Europe. Difficulties might arise, of course, in distinguishing a premeditated crisis, in which the main danger is a failure of deter-rence, from one which has arisen inadvertently, perhaps as a result of instability in Eastern Europe. The problem is compounded by the fact that, even in a crisis where one side is not deliberately challenging the adversary's commitment, an over-cautious policy could encourage the other side to become more assertive and start perceiving opportunities rather than dangers. The consequences of getting it wrong either way are considerable: a mismanaged and uncontrollable crisis in which events take on a logic and dynamism of their own, or a series of miscalculations resulting in a breakdown of deterrence and in one side's deliberately crossing the line between coercion and violence. The latter kind of failure was evident in British policy in the Falklands crisis in March 1982, while the most extreme case of the former – a crisis running out of control – was July 1914.

What makes this even more disturbing is that crises in Central Europe would almost certainly contain elements of both potential uncontrollability and weakened deterrence. Such crises require a particularly judicious blend of coercion and reassurance if they are to be successfully managed and defused. Since one cannot guarantee that the United States will get the balance right in relation to the reinforcement issue, there is no escape from this uncertainty. Nor is this necessarily a negative factor. Faced with such uncertainty, it seems unlikely that the Soviet Union would perceive itself as having sufficient military advantage in the Central Region to make an attack on Western Europe an attractive proposition. Defensive preparations near the intra-German border, supplemented by at least some limited moves towards defence in depth, would render it even less attractive. And this conclusion would almost certainly be strengthened when Soviet leaders take into account the nuclear component of NATO's military posture.

There has been considerable criticism in Europe of NATO's reliance on short-range battlefield nuclear weapons. Lawrence Freedman, for example, has argued very persuasively that there is no convincing military rationale for such forces; that they divert resources from conventional forces; and that they increase the dangers of premature escalation, making it more difficult to manage and contain hostilities if they occur.[23] For all this, one can argue that these systems still have important roles to play in NATO's order of battle. Far from being incompatible with the defensive preparations outlined above, they can actually strengthen their effect on deterrence. They act as an additional complicating factor in Soviet calculations. If the hazards of the European battlefield are substantial for the Soviet Union even before nuclear weapons are introduced into the equation, they are even more so after this is done. In order to launch a successful offensive, the Soviet Union must concentrate its forces in sufficient strength to make a decisive breakthrough. Yet massed forces make tempting targets for battlefield nuclear weapons, and although NATO might be inhibited from an early first use of such weapons, Moscow could not safely assume that this would be so. Indeed, if the checkerboard defence system succeeded in channelling the Soviet advance in particular directions, this would add to the vulnerability of the attacking forces to nuclear strikes. Another important function of battlefield nuclear weapons is the fact that they add to the escalatory potential inherent in any war in Europe: their impact is not to deny gains to the Soviet Union but to heighten the risks of aggression in Central Europe. Indeed, Bracken has identified three ways in which NATO's nuclear weapons give a high degree of credibility to what would otherwise be an incredible threat. 'Decentralized and delegated control of nuclear weapons once they are put on alert, the ambiguity of command authority over the employment of nuclear weapons, and the complexity of wartime and crisis management' all increase the possibility that the weapons would be used during hostilities in Europe.[24] This is not an unmixed blessing, of course, and it is once again necessary to balance competing criteria.

The trend certainly seems to be towards downgrading the importance of battlefield nuclear weapons. Yet it can be argued that although the reduction announced by the North Atlantic Council at its meeting in Canada in October 1983 was a tacit acknowledgment that NATO has traditionally placed too much reliance on these systems, there is also a danger of going too far in the opposite direction. Although the current phase of reductions will leave more than sufficient for NATO's needs, it is perhaps worth emphasizing that these forces are a significant element in the 'seamless web' of capabilities available to the Alliance, and act as an important link between conventional weapons and the long-range theatre nuclear forces. This is very different from seeing them as a substitute for conventional capabilities, as has sometimes been the case in the past.

Although destruction of NATO's nuclear stockpiles would be among the prime objectives of a Soviet conventional advance, there is little fear that these systems would undermine peacetime crisis management (as opposed to war limitation) in Europe. The deployment of cruise missiles and more especially Pershing IIs, by contrast, almost certainly adds to Moscow's fears about a NATO first strike against Soviet command and control centres. Bracken, in his incisive study of strategic command and control, has argued very persuasively that deployments which minimize the warning time available to either of the superpowers in a crisis could undermine attempts to maintain control and defuse the confrontation peacefully.[25] On the other hand, these long-range systems play a crucial role in 'coupling' any conflict in Europe to the possibility of a strategic exchange between the two superpowers. As Bracken has acknowledged, 'The geographic asymmetry of the European situation provides the linkage for escalating theater to a strategic war. Washington and New York are safe from theater nuclear destruction, but Moscow and Leningrad are not. It is hard to imagine that the Soviet Union would accept an artificial distinction between strategic and theater war if its High Command in Moscow were attacked by NATO nuclear weapons.'[26] Although it would be almost as difficult for an American president to initiate the use of long-range theatre nuclear forces against the Soviet homeland as it would be to order an intercontinental strike, the very deployment of these weapons in Europe brings them inescapably into the equation. And the fact that some of the missiles are deployed in forward rather than rear areas increases the chances of NATO's being faced with a 'use them or lose them' dilemma. Although this, like the presence of the short-range systems, adds to the escalatory potential of any conflict in Europe, it is not invariably a bad thing. Indeed, one of the ironies of the situation in Europe, as Raymond Aron pointed out some years ago, is that escalation is simultaneously a danger to be avoided and a threat to be used for deterrence purposes.[27] The benefits to be obtained from strengthened deterrence, therefore, have to be weighed against the added problems for crisis management and the increased difficulty of limiting hostilities once they erupt.

In this connection, suggestions for improving the crisis prevention and crisis management facilities that are available to the two superpowers have considerable relevance. A number of proposals have been made by senators such as Sam Nunn, John Warner and the late Henry Jackson, by former officials such as William Perry, and by analysts such as Barry Blechman and Alexander George.[28] Although there have been differences of emphasis from one proposal to another, there appears to be a growing consensus that separate crisis management centres in Moscow and Washinton are preferable to the creation of a single centre in, say, Geneva. Among the problems with the notion of a joint centre is that, despite its considerable symbolic importance, it would be remote from the decision-makers with the final responsibility, and would add an extra communications burden during periods when channels were already overloaded. In addition, a joint centre might be used to reassure the adversary as part of a comprehensive deception strategy.

Although separate centres in national capitals would mitigate these problems, the possibility that communications channels established for purposes of reassurance might be used to help conceal surprise attack can never be completely excluded. On balance, however, the risks appear to be worth taking in view of the possible benefits which might accrue to both superpowers. Along with the agreement on upgrading the hot line to include a capability for the speedy transfer of facsimile material such as maps, the centres could have both a substantive and a symbolic impact. In substantive terms, they could add to the possibility of early warning and consultation about emerging developments which appeared likely to precipitate tensions between the two superpowers. This would provide an opportunity for Moscow and Washington to use quiet diplomacy and avoid a direct clash. The less public the commitment of each side, the more flexible its position is likely to be. In symbolic terms, the establishment of crisis prevention and crisis management centres would be a welcome sign that, despite the reversion to Cold War rhetoric, Washington and Moscow still acknowledge their common interest in avoiding situations in which miscalculation or errors of judgment could precipitate hostilities that neither side really wants. Although the main crises for the centres would probably arise from events in the Third World, they would also be used for contingencies in Europe. In the event of a crisis in Eastern Europe, for example, the centres could help to reduce the possibility of misperception and misunderstanding that might surround Soviet preparations for intervention.

There seems little doubt, therefore, that the creation of crisis management centres in Washington and Moscow is highly desirable. For such centres to become an effective part of the decision-making process in either government, they would have to be staffed by high-ranking officials who had very close links with the key decision-makers themselves. In the United States, for example, such a centre could be staffed by key members of the National Security Council staff, together with senior figures from the State and Defense Departments.

However good the facilities in the two capitals, they would have to be supplemented by special arrangements for allied representation and consultation in the event of developments, either in Europe or elsewhere, which could propel NATO and the Warsaw Pact into a direct confrontation. Although the two superpowers would have the prime responsibility for crisis prevention and crisis management, additional consultative arrangements would be essential to reassure the allies that their interests would not be disregarded and problems settled over their heads. The experience of the early 1970s, when superpower agreements such as that on the Prevention of Nuclear War aroused considerable anxiety and suspicion on the part of the European allies, cautions against any Soviet–American arrangements which appear too exclusive. With the provision for some allied participation, however, the establishment of such centres could help to restore European confidence in the United States, and counter the image of a belligerent and irresponsible power which holds sway in certain portions of European opinion. This is not to suggest that the only value of such an initiative would be its public relations impact; on the contrary, it would be a practical step towards the kind of confidence-building which is an essential part of the attempt to regulate the 'adversary partnership' between Washington and Moscow. Such a step might have much more impact than renewed arms control negotiations which, with their continual emphasis on parity, seem to have become increasingly sterile, if not irrelevant.

All this may appear far removed from questions relating to the American military presence in Western Europe, but the connections are in fact very strong. Whatever shape NATO's military posture finally takes as a result of the current ferment over strategy and force structure, the fact that the superpower military confrontation is at its starkest in Europe suggests the need for some arrangements which will help to reduce the dangers and eliminate potential instabilities. And this is as important when there are 350,000 American troops in Europe as when there are only 50,000.

To argue in this way is not to imply that better arrangements for crisis prevention and crisis management can replace the more traditional concerns such as deterrence and defence. Nevertheless, such arrangements and other confidence-building measures can be an important supplement to these more orthodox means of achieving security. The

issue which must now be examined is whether or not there are any
feasible alternatives to the current levels of American troops in Western
Europe.

6 The implications of troop reductions

In considering the possible consequences of a smaller American military presence in Western Europe, one must identify not only the scale of any reductions but also the speed with which they might occur. There is also a crucial distinction between reductions which take place as a result of unilateral American decisions with little or no consultation with the allies, and reductions made as part of a coordinated attempt to reform the Alliance and change the distribution of roles, missions and responsibilities among the allies. The possibility of engineering such reforms is briefly explored in the final chapter. The emphasis in the present chapter is on the response of the Europeans to moves which are initiated by the United States but do not form part of any comprehensive reform of the Alliance.

Although there is perhaps a degree of redundancy in the existing level of American troops, as compared with the figures in the mid-1970s, any reduction which takes the figure significantly below 300,000 would have serious implications for the Alliance and would raise a variety of questions about NATO strategy and especially the relationship between deterrence and defence. Indeed, one of the problems is that certain groups and individuals in the United States appear to be increasingly hostile to any posture which demands that the President initiate the use of nuclear weapons on behalf of Western Europe. And the weaker the conventional forces available to NATO, the greater the reliance on the nuclear threat. If, therefore, a significant cut in US forces in Europe is not followed by European initiatives to compensate for the resulting gap in NATO's defensive capabilities, the United States would almost certainly be tempted to disengage completely. One of the dangers with limited US troop reductions is that they could develop a logic and momentum of their own. For the United States, the worst position of all would be a continuing commitment to European security which could be implemented only through the early use of nuclear weapons. Although proponents of troop reductions such as Henry Kissinger, Sam Nunn and Jeffrey Record base their position on the dangers of NATO's existing posture, the course they are advocating would be even more dangerous for the United States unless the European allies were galvanized into compensatory measures going far beyond their present efforts.[1] Without such efforts, substantial cuts of the kind discussed by Kissinger — and even the less drastic course advocated by Nunn — could lead eventually to a complete American military disengagement from Western Europe. If the dominant consideration for the United States is to minimize the nuclear dangers, reducing the number of troops in Europe is not the most obvious way to go about it! The existing level of forces at least provides limited conventional options, and although these options do not generate enormous confidence, at least they offer some prospect for the United States of its commitment to Europe being implemented at a tolerable cost. A reduction in troop levels which was not followed by European efforts to maintain the existing ratio of forces on the Central Front would confront the United States with much starker choices and could result in a far more fundamental reappraisal.

One of the main implications of this is that West European ability and willingness to compensate for any substantial reduction in US troops could be crucial in heading off further troop withdrawals. Yet if a substantial reduction would pose problems for the United States, it would pose equally difficult dilemmas for Western Europe. In particular, the Europeans would have to consider how seriously they regarded the Soviet threat, and what efforts they were prepared to make to meet it in view of the other demands on resources.

To some extent, the Europeans have been able to be fairly sanguine about the Soviet threat precisely because the United States has been unequivocally involved in underwriting West European security. Should this degree of involvement change, then the allies would have to confront the issue much more directly than has hitherto been necessary. There are several possible responses, depending upon what view of Moscow one holds.

If one believes that the Soviet Union is obsessed by security concerns of its own and has much more to lose than to gain from any deterioration of its relationship with Western Europe, then there would be little incentive to take compensatory measures. And if Soviet intransigence is largely a product of the threat posed by the United States, a reduction in the American military presence could reassure Moscow and thereby improve, rather than undermine, stability in Europe. On the other hand, if it were followed by a significant increase in European military preparations or by an attempt to establish a more cohesive European defence identity in which the Federal Republic played a larger part, then any reassurance would be more than offset by the anxieties this would provoke in Moscow – and possibly in several West European states too. In other words, if one's view of Soviet military capabilities is that they are primarily a response to a perceived threat, the tendency would be to do nothing to fill the gap caused by a reduction in US force levels. On the contrary, the main thrust of policy would be to improve relations further with Moscow. The emphasis would be on promoting détente rather than enhancing deterrence. The difficulty is that this would further alienate the United States from Western Europe and render Washington even less willing to maintain its security commitment.

The opposite view of the Soviet Union – that it is essentially a predatory state, held in check only by countervailing power – would lead to a much more vigorous attempt to fill the gap left by a partial withdrawal of US forces, in order to head off any further reductions. Although such a possibility could not be ruled out, the problem is that West European governments would run up against the same political and economic constraints which currently make it difficult for them to satisfy American demands for greater burden-sharing. The sense of urgency, however, would almost certainly be much greater than it is with the existing American presence, and a higher level of sacrifice would possibly be accepted as essential. It is not inconceivable that governments might decide to devote the level of resources to defence that the United States has long been urging. The incentives for greater defence cooperation would also be stronger. Nevertheless, even if West European governments were anxious to fill the gap left in NATO's conventional posture as a result of an American troop cut, the difficulties would be formidable.

The implications of troop reductions

It is hard to predict what level of resources governments would be prepared to devote to defence. In this connection, one cannot ignore the failure of the European governments to meet the annual 3 per cent real increase in defence budgets agreed upon by the Alliance in 1977 and 1978. The 1983 report to Congress on Allied Contributions to the Common Defense included a summary of the average increases in expenditure for the years from 1979 to 1982. In 1979, the weighted average increase for all NATO nations (excluding the United States) was 2.2 per cent. In both 1980 and 1981, it was 2.7 per cent, and in 1982 it fell to somewhere between 1 and 1.6 per cent and continued at about this level in 1983. Furthermore, the aggregate increase for 1982 hid the fact that West Germany, Greece, Turkey and Portugal all had defence budgets which in real terms were declining.[2] This suggests that the greater willingness to meet the 3 per cent target in the immediate aftermath of Afghanistan was merely a temporary increase undertaken reluctantly and as a result of American pressure. Although a reduction in US troops could have a more substantial and more lasting impact on European defence budgets than the Soviet intervention in Afghanistan, the problems of allocating resources among competing demands and requirements would remain at least as intense as they have been in recent years. Indeed, the difficulties could worsen. There are problems at all levels of the resource allocation process: the total level of government spending, the competition for funds within the public sector of the European economies, and the distribution of resources within defence.[3]

There is no doubt that most West European governments are motivated by the desire to keep public spending under control. Concern with the prospects for the revival of industry after the recession of the early 1980s means that they will be anxious to minimize the tax burden in the corporate sector of their economies through the rest of the decade. Even if there is an upturn in the West European economies, therefore, there will not be a corresponding increase in the extra resources available to the public sector. And, given the vulnerability of the advanced industrialized economies to increases in the price of oil, the recovery from the recession could prove to be fragile at best. The implication of all this is that the resources available for all public purposes in the years ahead will be limited, either as a result of sluggish growth, or as a consequence of government economic policies.

In these circumstances the competition for scarce resources will be particularly intense, and defence budgets are unlikely to emerge unscathed. The social welfare budgets of most European members of NATO have come under considerable strain in recent years. The desire of governments to maintain the welfare state and compensate for the restrictions that have been placed on spending for health, education and welfare means that the pressures on defence ministries to make economies could well increase. That is not necessarily undesirable. In contrast to the Reagan Administration, most European governments conceive of security in very broad terms, regarding it as far more than protection against Soviet aggression. The internal fabric of West European security is as important as the external dimension, and social stability is as vital an ingredient as military strength.[4] Furthermore, as governments have to contend with ageing populations and increased unemployment, the internal imperatives of legitimation will almost certainly require greater expenditure on social welfare. At the very least, the scope for savings in areas other than defence will be minimal. In other words, economic recovery will not necessarily ease pressures on the defence budgets of most West European states. The North Atlantic Council has failed to maintain the 3 per cent target for 1985 and 1986, and even in Britain, with a conservative government committed to a strong defence effort, the pledge to maintain a 3 per cent per annum real increase has been abandoned after 1985/6.

The British example illustrates another problem related both to resource allocation and to the issue of compensation for an American troop reduction. There would not necessarily be agreement on the form that compensation should take. At a time when the emphasis in the Alliance is on strengthening conventional forces, both the United Kingdom and France are engaged in expensive modernization programmes for their strategic forces. And although the British government has claimed that the impact of the Trident acquisition on the defence budget will be limited, the opportunity costs within defence can hardly be ignored. Although a reduction in the American troop level in Europe would strengthen the existing rationale for Trident as a hedge against an uncertain future in which the American guarantee to Europe could be eroded, it would also demand a greater conventional effort. Trident would do nothing to fill the gap in NATO's defences on the Central

Front. On the contrary, the United Kingdom, seeing a reduced troop presence as a manifestation of a weakening American nuclear guarantee, could decide to give its strategic programme a much higher priority, at the expense of conventional forces. American troop reductions could even encourage a reappraisal of Britain's own continental commitment.

It is not inconceivable, therefore, that the British reaction could create further anxieties in Washington about the viability of NATO's conventional posture. This, in turn, would pose dilemmas for Britain about whether the most appropriate security policy was one in which the emphasis was on its links with the United States or with Western Europe. Although British foreign policy in the postwar period is sometimes interpreted as an inexorable move towards Europe, this move has been at the expense of the UK's global role; the relationship with the United States has not suffered. Indeed, British policy has been explicitly designed to avoid the stark choice between continental ties and the connection with Washington. But in the event of a substantial reduction of American troops, such a choice could become inescapable.

This is not to suggest that an enhancement of Britain's nuclear capability is inconsistent with continued concern over security and stability in Europe. Many of those who argue for reform of NATO give considerable attention to the need for *European* nuclear deterrent forces, which could be based on the existing or projected capabilities of Britain and France. Yet this idea is one that has consistently – if tacitly – been opposed by the United States. Indeed, there is something in the argument that successive administrations in Washington have been content to extend the nuclear deterrent over Western Europe only so long as the Europeans accepted American primacy in nuclear planning. Although some breaches of this were acceptable, and Washington gradually learned to live with the French *force de dissuasion*, a coordination of British and French strategic forces is unlikely to be regarded with equanimity by the United States. The price of American nuclear protection is that the President should have maximum discretion in determining how that guarantee would be implemented in the event of Soviet aggression against Western Europe. In the event of a reduction in US forces being followed by moves towards Anglo-French nuclear cooperation, there could be considerable pressure for further American disengagement. The less control American policy-makers are able to exert over the actions of their NATO allies in a crisis in Europe, the less attractive will they perceive the US commitment to be.

To some extent this might be offset by the actions of the Federal Republic. The Bonn government, as NATO's front-line state, would have considerable interest in compensating for a reduction in US troops deployed on its territory. On the other hand, the Federal Republic has to contend with the same constraints and pressures that inhibit the defence programmes and policies of the other European allies. As one study noted: 'Domestic constraints on strengthening the conventional forces have increased dramatically, even though pressures to reduce reliance on the nuclear leg of the NATO triad have never been greater . . . In West Germany the future of flexible response and the associated role of conventional defence will depend on some critical variables: the fiscal priorities of the government, trends in the defence budget (especially in procurement), the supply of manpower for the Bundeswehr, the state of the economy, and the domestic consensus on budget priorities.'[5]

Although the sense of urgency generated by a substantial American troop cut might well provide the impetus for overcoming some of these constraints, there would almost certainly still be strict limits on what the Federal Republic could do to compensate for the gap in NATO's conventional posture resulting from reductions in the American military presence in Europe. The declining birth rate, for example, means that there will be an almost inevitable manpower shortfall in the second half of the 1980s. There are a number of ways in which this difficulty can be partly overcome — such as extending the length of military service, conscripting women or reducing the standards for conscripts — but it is difficult to dissent from the conclusion that 'the coming shortage of conscripts and reservists means that there will be no pool of personnel from which to form additional combat units in the forseeable future.'[6]

In addition to these familiar constraints there are peculiarities in Bonn's own history and position which add further problems. In the event of an American troop reduction, the dilemmas facing the Federal Republic would be acute and unprecedented. On the one hand, a need would almost certainly be felt to take action to compensate for the diminution in NATO's military strength. On the other hand, there would be considerable reluctance to take action which would antagonize Moscow. This reluctance should not simply be dismissed as evidence of

Finlandization. It would merely be a recognition that the basis for security and stability in Europe goes beyond military preparedness. As discussed in Chapter 5, deterrence and defence have to be balanced by measures designed to build confidence between the two halves of Europe. The problem is, of course, that if the Federal Republic failed to initiate compensatory measures, this again would add to its poor image in the United States, thereby encouraging further reductions in the remaining American presence. Consequently, Bonn would have to tread a narrow and difficult path in which the needs of an Ostpolitik which had become both more delicate and more vital than ever before would have to be weighed against the needs of the Westpolitik and the desire to retain a residual American commitment. In these circumstances it is not obvious that Bonn would have either the will or the capacity to fill the gap left by the reduction in American forces. Although the reasons would be different from those of Britain, the final result could well be the same.

In the light of this, the French reaction takes on even more significance. The problem, of course, is that France, having attempted to distance itself politically from NATO's integrated military organization in 1966, would be unlikely to reintegrate its forces. Yet the impact of this should not be exaggerated. France, after all, is still a member of the Alliance and, equally important, still maintains a substantial military presence in the Federal Republic. Furthermore, other allies also have considerable discretion in determining at what point in a crisis in Europe their forces assigned to SACEUR would actually come under his command. In other words, the French position is far from anomalous. In addition, the French decision to create a Rapid Action Force which will 'potentially be able to participate in the reinforcement of allied capabilities' could augment the capacity for conventional defence.[7] Even so, the priority for France is still its own independent nuclear forces, and with the refurbishment of both tactical and strategic systems, there is unlikely to be much surplus in the defence budget for conventional forces. It may well be that the Rapid Action Force can fulfil its potential only at the expense of existing conventional units. In other words, although France might be in a slightly better position than either Britain or the Federal Republic to initiate measures to compensate for a cut in US troops, it is still likely to face significant constraints.

If the three major West European powers are either unwilling or unable to increase their defence efforts to the extent necessary to compensate for a reduction in the American presence, it would be unrealistic to expect the smaller allies to fill the gap. Part of the reason is that they suffer from the same kind of resource and manpower problems as Britain, France and the Federal Republic. In these circumstances, a certain amount of buck-passing would be almost inevitable. A failure of the larger powers to take the necessary action to maintain NATO's conventional strength would have a negative effect on the attitude of countries like Belgium, Holland and Denmark. Looking to their more powerful neighbours for initiatives which were not forthcoming, they could very easily slip into apathy. If London, Paris and Bonn no longer appeared to take European security problems seriously, the incentives for the smaller European states to do so would be minimal. They would not believe their efforts could make much difference, and so they would be reluctant to make major sacrifices for what could only be regarded as a lost cause.

It is possible, therefore, that, far from galvanizing the Europeans into more vigorous defence efforts, a reduction in the American presence could encourage a much more defeatist attitude. In these circumstances, there would be a considerable temptation for the European allies to improve relations with Moscow, not out of a concern for maintaining détente or enhancing stability, but simply out of weakness. As a result, negotiation could all too easily become supplication. Once again, this would merely confirm American policy-makers and legislators in their worst suspicions about the European allies and provoke further reductions in the US presence in Europe. The overall result could be a downward spiral in the Atlantic relationship, and an American disengagement.

Another reason for such a gloomy prognosis is that American troop reductions which do not galvanize the Europeans into doing more would leave NATO even more dependent on the early use of nuclear weapons than it is now. Being committed to such an option on behalf of unreliable allies is not a position that the United States would particularly enjoy. On the other hand, if Washington reduced troops as part of an attempt to rationalize its global defence posture, and if the Europeans were able to provide positive evidence that they were making efforts to compensate for the shortfall (perhaps through a programme for defensive preparations of the kind outlined in Chapter 5), then the United States might be more willing to maintain its commitment. Indeed, if Washington reduced conventional forces but continued to deploy somewhere in the region of 4,000 short-range theatre nuclear weapons, as well as 572 ground-launched cruise missiles and Pershing IIs, there would not necessarily be a reduction in the credibility of its nuclear guarantee to Western Europe.

This conclusion runs against the conventional wisdom and challenges part of the rationale for maintaining US troops in Europe at the existing levels. A major function of their presence is to act as hostages to ensure American involvement in any conflict on the Continent, but this is not dependent on a particular level of forces. As Senator Mansfied argued, if American troops in Europe are intended simply to link the fate of Europe to the American nuclear guarantee, then this could be accomplished at much lower force levels than currently exist. So long as there are sufficient US troops deployed in Western Europe to ensure that Soviet aggression very obviously and very rapidly puts Moscow on a collision course with Washington, this may be adequate to deter Soviet leaders. Deterrence in Europe does not require the United States coolly and rationally to initiate nuclear war on behalf of its allies; it requires simply that there should be enough American forces in Europe to ensure that in the event of Soviet aggression there would be a direct superpower confrontation which would far surpass the Cuban missile crisis in its intensity.

The hallmark of such confrontations is that neither side can maintain complete control over the situation; events and actions can very easily generate a logic and momentum of their own. Therefore, although the NATO strategy of flexible response emphasizes limited and controlled escalation, it is arguable that the possibility of inadvertent escalation is far more important. And so long as there is a substantial (and the vagueness of the term may be advantageous) American presence in which there is close integration of conventional and nuclear forces, this possibility is a very real one. Indeed, Bracken's arguments about the problems of controlling theatre nuclear forces once they have been dispersed are particularly relevant here. As he put it, 'What some observers see as a thoughtless and disorderly development of highly differentiated nuclear forces is in fact precisely the kind of force structure needed for a deterrence strategy whose implementation would be suicidal.'[8] In this sense, deterrence in Europe rests upon what Schelling described as 'threats that leave something to chance'.[9] In an era of strategic parity, the Soviet Union may no longer be certain that the United States would initiate a suicidal nuclear exchange on behalf of Western Europe. But Moscow would still regard a conflict in Europe as involving incalculable risks of escalation to the point at which one or both sides might feel that such exchanges were inevitable and initiate them before the adversary could do so. Even though the United States, behaving rationally, would attempt to avoid such an outcome, there is no guarantee that it could succeed. A war in Europe could itself prove to be an irrational process.

Although Moscow, and indeed the Europeans, might find it hard to believe that the United States would make a rational decision to fight a nuclear war on Europe's behalf, it strains their credulity far less to assume that such an outcome could be the result of a complex and uncontrollable sequence of events which begins with Soviet and American forces meeting on the European battlefield. After all, one of the consequences of hostilities in Europe would be that both superpowers would place their strategic nuclear forces on alert. In these circumstances, the possibility that one side might interpret the other's precautionary moves as preparation for attack could not be dismissed – especially where each side's warning and alert system has become enormously sensitive to that of the adversary.[10] In other words, the crucial threshold in Europe is not between conventional and nuclear war but between peace and war. What Bernard Brodie once described as the clarity of the choice between non-war and destruction in Europe retains its salience.[11] Once this line is crossed, the outcome is unforeseeable – and the only certainty is that the risks are immense.

There are two other considerations which strengthen the argument that even though the American nuclear guarantee to Western Europe is no longer absolute, it is still credible. The first is that insofar as super-power crises are competitions in risk-taking, their outcome tends to be determined primarily by a balance of interests: the superpower with most at stake will almost invariably be prepared to run higher risks than the one with less. It is arguable that this is a far more important deter-minant of relative resolve than is the balance of either conventional or strategic power. And in any crisis over Western Europe the United States would almost certainly have a greater stake in keeping its allies free from Soviet domination than the Soviet Union would have in subjugating them. Although the usual question is whether or not the United States would sacrifice New York for London, Paris or Bonn, this is not the real issue. A much more important question is, 'Why should the Soviet Union risk Moscow for London, Paris or Bonn?' There are few reasons for thinking that the Soviet Union would take greater risks to obtain control over Western Europe than the United States would be prepared to take to ensure that its European allies remained free and independent of Moscow. The American interest in denying the Soviet Union access to the resources of Western Europe will remain as significant in the future as it has been in the past, even if Washington reduces its military presence by half. After all, a successful Soviet attack on Western Europe would almost certainly make the Soviet Union the dominant power in the international system and, psychologically if not physically, relegate the United States to second place. Should Moscow succeed in challenging as vital an American commitment as that in Europe, then American pledges elsewhere would be rendered meaningless, and although a Fortress America would still be able to compete with Moscow, the sacrifices required would be far greater than at present. Indeed, Soviet domination of Western Europe would compel the United States to develop a permanent war economy – hardly a palatable proposition.

The second important consideration is that American troops in Europe represent an irrevocable commitment to the security of Europe. Although it could be plausibly argued that the larger the presence, the stronger the commitment, it could equally well be argued that there is considerable redundancy in the American military presence in the sense that the very deployment of troops in Germany would give the United States no other choice than to confront Soviet forces in the event of Warsaw Pact aggression. There is of course an irreducible minimum for such a presence. Should the troops be reduced to a level at which it would be feasible to withdraw them very rapidly in the event of a crisis, then their value as a symbol of the US commitment would be significantly reduced if not wholly undermined. As long, however, as there are sufficient troops to ensure that this is not an option and to make clear that the United States remains concerned about the security of Europe, deterrence seems unlikely to be weakened.

If Washington accepts that it is the inevitability of superpower confrontation, with all the risks which this entails, that is the key to deterrence in Europe, then the size and strength of its conventional contingent, while still important, need no longer be the crucial element in West European security. Consequently, the United States could make some reduction in its forces with impunity. Although this could run into the problem of appearing to go back towards reliance on a tripwire, in a sense it is simply a recognition that the American nuclear guarantee is far less fragile than much recent discussion has assumed. There has been a crisis of extended deterrence since the mid-1960s, and possibly since Sputnik. Yet there has been no evidence that the Soviet Union is any more willing to threaten the *status quo* in Europe now than in the period when Washington had overwhelming nuclear superiority. The nuclear guarantee may not be adequate to reassure the West Europeans, but it is almost certainly sufficient to deter the Russians. Deterrence does not depend upon the balance of conventional forces on the Central Front. Although this goes against much of the current orthodoxy, it merely reflects the fact that despite pretensions to being a collective defence organization, NATO is essentially a guarantee pact. Once this is acknowledged, the precise number of US troops in Europe becomes less significant.

This is not to deny that the European allies would oppose any substantial troop reduction. So long as this were accomplished on a phased basis over several years, however, it need not be too disruptive. Indeed, it could end the constant sniping over the size of the presence, ease the pressure on American forces elsewhere, and possibly even elicit some compensatory measures from the Europeans. And it might well be the one thing which would push the Federal Republic into accepting the necessity for non-provocative fixed defences near the intra-German border. The impact of the reduction could also be eased if the United States took some precautionary measures to facilitate a quick return of the troops in an emergency. Reliance on prepositioning equipment and rotation of the manpower to go with it, which began after the trilateral negotiations between Britain, the United Sates and West Germany in 1966-7, could be extended further. A reduction of troops could be compensated to some extent by an increased reliance on an expanded POMCUS (i.e., prepositioning of matériel configured to unit sets) programme, whereby equipment is available for reinforcements arriving from the continental United States. This would require that the Congress appropriate the funds for additional POMCUS stocks − something that could not be taken for granted, given past difficulties in obtaining adequate provision for the POMCUS programme.[12] The key issue, though, as suggested in Chapter 5, is less the capability for rapid reinforcement than the will to initiate the process in a crisis. Yet this problem already exists, and although it would be intensified by reductions in the American military presence in Europe, the difference would be one of degree rather than kind.

The implication of all this is that if the United States reduced forces in Europe as part of an attempt to cope with the problem of extensive commitments and limited resources, and did so on the understanding that this would lead to greater reliance on threats that leave something to chance than on a capacity for a sustained collective defence, there is no reason why the remaining presence should not be politically viable and strategically credible. And although this presence would not be dependent upon European attempts to compensate for the reduction, the American initiative might nevertheless have a salutary affect by encouraging attempts to initiate a fortification programme and strengthen active and reserve forces, albeit within the budgetary and manpower constraints identified above. Even if the Europeans were unwilling or unable to devote more resources to defence, they could at least attempt to make more efficient use of existing resources. In this way they might be able to go some way towards offsetting the gap in NATO's conventional defences.

Although this might appear a somewhat optimistic scenario, it recognizes that while the United States will remain committed to Europe for compelling reasons of self-interest, Washington also needs a degree of discretion on how that commitment is manifested in peacetime that hitherto the Europeans have been reluctant to acknowledge or accept. Yet if the reductions were carried out in a phased and orderly manner, and if they were accompanied by intensive consultations to prevent acrimony within the Alliance, they need not be debilitating. The one thing they would do is undermine the prospect for a successful conventional defence of Western Europe, but it can be argued that a Soviet conventional incursion is such a remote contingency that this does not matter a great deal. So long as the United States reaffirms its commitment, the Soviet Union seems unlikely to challenge it, just because there are fewer troops. As Paul Bracken has argued, 'The risks of escalation to all-out nuclear war are higher in Europe than anywhere else. No one has offered a convincing rationale for why the Soviet Union would initiate military activity there in order to advance its national interests. If war is a continuation of politics by other means, then the European stand-off of the past thirty-five years shows us that no Soviet political objective would ever justify the risks of undertaking large-scale military activity there.'[13]

Closely related to this is the fact that although there has been considerable discussion in Europe and the United States about the credibility of the American commitment, the Soviet Union has never given any indication that it regards this as in any way in doubt. The compelling feature of the postwar security system in Western Europe has been the *de facto* division into spheres of interest, and Soviet foreign policy has consistently worked within the limits this arrangement has imposed. For Moscow the American commitment has taken on many of the qualities of an international norm. The Soviet Union has always been far more concerned about Eastern Europe than about Western Europe and, in return for its acceptance of American influence over the Western part of the Continent, has wanted simple reciprocity. The great benefit of détente for the Soviet Union was that it helped to legitimize the *status quo* in Europe. The treaties with West Germany and the Helsinki Final Act were particularly important in this connection. To acknowledge this is not to argue that the Soviet Union always acts as a *status quo* power. There have been occasions when its behaviour outside Europe has revealed that it has revisionist and perhaps revolutionary aspirations. In Europe, however, there have been few signs that it is dissatisfied with the existing security arrangements. And even outside Europe the most striking feature of Soviet policy has been its caution. Apart from the installation of missiles in Cuba in 1962, the Soviet Union has not taken high risks. Its actions in Angola, the Horn of Africa and Afghanistan in the 1970s were not high-risk ventures in any sense. It was aware in all cases that the United States was unable or unwilling to make any moves to counteract its initiatives. American domestic politics, especially the backlash from Vietnam and Watergate, had effectively prohibited any US involvement in areas which were not of vital interest — and had

71

thereby given the Soviet Union a free hand. Although Soviet behaviour in the future will not necessarily be the same as in the past, there is little to suggest that Moscow will become more assertive or aggressive in its stance towards Western Europe, even if the American presence is reduced.

There are two main reasons for this conclusion. In the first place, the existing arrangements have certain advantages for Moscow. Although the Soviet Union regards some of the current manifestations of the American presence — especially the Pershing IIs in Germany — with distaste and possibly even alarm, the presence is almost certainly accepted as something which has positive benefits for Moscow. It is an important guarantor of the postwar security arrangements: American military forces in the Federal Republic act as an important constraint on Bonn. As Lawrence Freedman has noted, 'Europe has a history of turbulence and is, from a Soviet perspective, still politically fragile. The American presence can be seen as an important stabilizing influence which, if removed, would open the way for more dangerous forces — especially German|revanchism.'[14] Insofar as US troops are deployed in Europe as part of the solution to the German problem, they are not unwelcome to the Soviet Union. Containment, after all, can work in more than one direction. In addition to this, American troops in Western Europe help to legitimize Soviet hegemony in Eastern Europe.

A second reason why the Soviet Union seems unlikely to adopt a more overtly aggressive stance towards Western Europe is that such an approach has always proved counter-productive in the past. Actions by Moscow which appear to threaten NATO almost invariably provoke the Alliance into greater defence efforts and into adopting a more united front. Although Afghanistan was in some ways an exception, in that it had a divisive rather than a unifying impact, this was largely because the Soviet intervention was in a remote area which appeared irrelevant to European concerns.

All this is not to deny that the Soviet Union would like to become the dominant power in Europe or that in the long term it would prefer to see the countervailing power of the United States removed from the Continent. Nevertheless, these are long-term aspirations which, arguably, have little relevance to the short and medium terms. Indeed, in the short term, Moscow would almost certainly look on any precipitate reduction in American troops in Europe with considerable alarm. Although a gradual reduction in American force levels would be tolerable, and perhaps even welcome, any steps which triggered moves towards a more cohesive and vigorous West European defence identity or greater West German defence efforts would be regarded with apprehension. In fact the prospects for either of these developments coming about as a result of an American troop reduction are probably far more remote than Moscow fears. Nevertheless, the very fact that such possibilities exist would almost certainly encourage Soviet prudence. If American troops remained in Europe in numbers which were substantial, but also substantially less than at present, Moscow would have even greater incentive for caution. As Adam Ulam has argued, 'the Soviet nightmare is that Western Europe will unite politically and rearm itself vigorously, thereby leaving the Soviet Union facing two superpowers instead of one'.[15] Probably the only circumstances in which there would be moves towards political unification and sufficient rearmament to compensate for American troop reductions are those in which the United States appeared to be going and the Soviet Union to be coming. An American troop reduction by itself would probably be insufficient to generate the actions needed. And Soviet behaviour would almost certainly be tailored to ensure that the Europeans did not feel it necessary to move in this direction.

Much of this is extremely unfashionable. Nevertheless, it merely suggests that the military balance in Central Europe is only one element in the security arrangements in Europe, and that as soon as political considerations are introduced into the equation, there is far greater stability, and greater freedom of manoeuvre, than is usually assumed. Although the obvious counter to this is that intentions can change very suddenly, and that therefore the adversary's capabilities must be the basis for planning, there are equally, if not more, serious dangers in what can all too easily degenerate into oversimplified worst-case thinking. Deducing the adversary's intentions from his capabilities locks one into military confrontation to such an extent that opportunities for moderating and improving relations will be overlooked.

None of this means that the Europeans can afford to be sanguine about troop reductions. Indeed, there are compelling reasons for suggesting that the Alliance structure needs to be refashioned in certain respects, with the European allies taking on a greater degree of responsibility. Some of the possibilities for moving in this direction are explored in the next chapter.

7 Conclusions and recommendations

Questions regarding the American military presence in Western Europe are obviously of considerable importance in their own right. Equally significant, however, is the fact that they place into focus many of the broader issues involved in the Atlantic relationship and its future evolution. One of the paradoxes of this relationship is that the kind of actions which are required to demonstrate to Washington that the Europeans are good allies are the very actions that will lessen European dependence on the United States. At times in the past, a closer identity among the West Europeans has been regarded by some as incompatible with continued harmony in the Atlantic relationship. Similarly, there has been a muted strand in European opinion suggesting that the Europeans should not do more for defence lest this should enable the United States to do less. These arguments cannot simply be dismissed. There are forms of European cooperation, especially on nuclear matters, which the United States might not welcome. Nevertheless, it seems clear that the dangers for the Atlantic Alliance lie in the Europeans contributing less rather than more, and in stagnation rather than creativity. As Kissinger noted: 'Everyone has been afraid to take the initiative in changing the present arrangement, lest doing so unravel the whole enterprise. But since drift will surely lead to unraveling — if more imperceptibly — statesmanship demands a new approach.'[1]

The real difficulties, however, concern the form this new approach should take. An added problem is that there are at least three distinct areas in which changes are necessary: Alliance strategy, Alliance structure (which includes the distribution of roles and responsibilities) and Alliance relations with the Soviet Union. The difficulties are compounded by the complex interrelationships between each of these areas. Even taking them separately, however, the problems are immense. The very differences which have bedevilled the Alliance throughout much of its history also make agreement on certain reforms highly unlikely. The obstacles will be greater still if the initiatives come exclusively from the United States and reflect only American concerns and aspirations.

Kissinger's proposals suffer, in part at least, from such ethnocentrism. This is particularly the case with his demands for changes in strategy which would transform NATO into a collective defence organization and downgrade the American nuclear guarantee. Such a proposal appears to be an attempt to reduce the nuclear risks for the United States at the expense of the Europeans. Furthermore, there is a basic incongruity in Kissinger's arguments, in that he emphasizes the need for the Europeans to take a greater share of the responsibilities, as well as the burdens, of Alliance security, but then defines these responsibilities for them in an extremely restrictive way. By advocating that the Europeans focus almost exclusively on conventional defence, he is condemning them to permanent second-class status within the Alliance. In doing so, he is making the same mistake as Robert McNamara did in the early 1960s, with his demands for greater European conventional capabilities and his criticism of European deterrent forces. The idea that Europe become a second and more equal pillar in the Atlantic Alliance is an attractive one; recommending that this be done solely through European conventional forces undermines it. Indeed, if Europe is to become a more mature partner of the United States, then greater efforts will have to be made at the nuclear level as well as the conventional.

This is not to belittle the importance of conventional forces. In fact there is considerable evidence that the European governments ·take seriously the concerns voiced by both the United States and their own populations about NATO's heavy reliance on nuclear weapons. In the NATO Defence Ministers' meeting of May 1984, it was agreed to develop a range of high-technology weapon systems and to increase spending on NATO infrastructure so as to facilitate and protect American reinforcements deploying to Europe in an emergency. Although this was a step in the right direction, it was almost a routine response to American pressure. Western Europe needs to go beyond incrementalism of this kind — valuable as it is — and adopt a more far-reaching and better publicized set of proposals. These should include provision for fixed defences as well as further willingness to go along the ET road – albeit without the deep-strike elements that have hitherto dominated much of the discussion. There are other measures, such as the augmentation of ammunition stocks and the creation of additional reserves, which should also be incorporated into the programme. Although stocks and reserves are not particularly exciting, they are certainly not insignificant in military terms. Furthermore, ammunition is one of the areas for greater European contribution identified by the Nunn Amendment and the Cohen compromise. Inclusion of this element in the package, therefore, might help to contain further congressional demands for American troop withdrawals from Western Europe.

Insofar as the initiative could also be an exercise in public relations, the Europeans could highlight the extent of their defence efforts in recent years. Although they have not performed particularly well in terms of defence spending, they have taken on greater burdens in certain areas. The Host Nation Support Agreement, signed between Washington and Bonn in 1982, is a prime example of this, with the Federal Republic agreeing to provide 93,000 reservists, in the event of an emergency in Europe, to support American forward-deployed forces and early re-inforcements.[2] Another example is the Washington–Bonn agreement of July 1984 on joint air defence. The Europeans could also continue to emphasize that they provide the bulk of the conventional forces in Europe. As a 1983 Congressional Research Service report pointed out: 'Of the ready forces currently available in Europe, about 91 per cent of the ground forces and 86 per cent of the air forces come from European countries, as do 75 per cent of NATO's tanks and more than 90 per cent of its armored divisions.'[3] With an agreement which consisted of a reduction in American troops in Europe and greater European efforts to create a viable defence line close to the intra-German border, the figures would look even more favourable to Europe. Another advantage of a smaller American military presence is that it would be politically viable and less likely to generate resentment and criticism. As Senator Claiborne Pell has argued; 'to diminish the American presence within the framework of a broad review and reaffirmation of collective commitment could instill new will in the Alliance itself'.[4]

There would, of course, be considerable difficulties, in establishing an appropriate institutional base for this kind of review if the Europeans themselves were to take the lead. Although the Eurogroup – an informal grouping of European members of NATO – proved particularly useful in the burden-sharing disputes of the early 1970s, the absence of France renders this forum unsatisfactory. There might be considerable merit, therefore, in using the Western European Union (WEU) – whose membership consists of France, West Germany, the United Kingdom, Italy and the Benelux countries – for such a review. This has particular attraction in view of renewed French interest in the WEU as a vehicle for greater European defence cooperation. Although France appears to be responding to concerns about both American unilateralism and West German neutralism, the resuscitation of the WEU might nevertheless provide the opportunity for bringing France closer to NATO and thereby increase the prospects for a second pillar within the Atlantic framework. The historical experience of schemes for European defence cooperation cautions against great expectations, but the current upsurge of enthusiasm differs from previous episodes in that France no longer appears to be promoting a 'European Europe' as an alternative to an 'Atlantic Europe'. Instead, European defence cooperation is seen as perfectly consistent with the Alliance framework in the short and medium terms, and as a hedge against the dissolution of the Alliance in the long term.

If the position of France is crucial, so too is that of the Federal Republic. The enthusiastic participation of Bonn is essential. Yet West Germany is particularly sensitive to the views of both superpowers. Consequently, the exercise could be made more palatable – and indeed more important – if it incorporated a comprehensive study concerned with East-West relations and the whole question of out-of-area issues. By accepting much broader terms of reference than were evident in the Eurogroup's activities in the early 1970s, a European grouping would have an opportunity to make far-reaching proposals for the Alliance. Although a comprehensive agenda of this kind might appear formidable, it could be rendered more manageable by establishing a series of working groups with responsibility for each of the main issues. Furthermore, while the initial analysis would be done exclusively by the Europeans, there would be opportunities for US representatives to have an input, so that when the recommendations were finally tabled in NATO, they would not be a further source of European–American discord.

The studies would be based upon several propositions: that the Atlantic Alliance remains the most appropriate body for dealing with threats to the security of Western Europe and North America; that the Europeans have to take a greater share of responsibilities as well as burdens; that Western Europe cannot be indifferent to instabilities and potential threats outside Europe; that the existing level of American forces in Europe is not sacrosanct; and that security depends on far more than military strength and ever-increasing levels of defence spending. Starting from these premises, the Europeans would consider a number of key issues. These might include: the possibility of a geographical division of labour in which the United States acts on behalf of the West outside Europe, while the Europeans themselves take over the responsibility for their security in Europe; Kissinger's idea that there should be a reversal of the traditional pattern whereby the Supreme Allied Commander Europe is an American and the NATO Secretary-General is a European; and the need for a more comprehensive security policy towards the Soviet Union in which crisis prevention procedures and confidence-building measures complement deterrence and defence. Although these ideas cannot be fully dealt with here, it is possible to make some preliminary observations.

In recent years there has been a gradual, if grudging, recognition by NATO Europe that its security is dependent upon events outside Europe as well as upon what happens on the Continent itself. American demands for compensation, facilitation and participation in out-of-area operations have elicited a more positive response than is often acknowledged. Consideration has been given to ways in which the Europeans might compensate for the diversion of American reinforcements in the United States to the Persian Gulf, and American deployments in the Indian Ocean have been facilitated by the use of Diego Garcia, owned by Britain. In addition, Britain and France still have obligations and force deployments beyond the European theatre. In short, the United States does not have a monopoly of the burden outside Europe. And although the arrangements for dealing with out-of-area contingencies have been *ad hoc* and not entirely satisfactory, they are preferable to a more formal division of labour in which the United States acts alone outside Europe, while the allies take the primary responsibility for their own defence in Europe.

Some moves in that direction may be inevitable, but it is important not to go too far. There are several reasons for this. First, there are sometimes important differences of appreciation and assessment between the United States and Western Europe, which suggests that entrusting Washington with a monopoly of decision-making on out-of-area issues affecting the Alliance might not be appropriate. There might be some interests that the Europeans can look after rather more effectively than the United States. Second, many out-of-area problems require a comprehensive approach in which diplomacy, economic assistance and military support all have a part to play. The Europeans have as much to offer in terms of diplomacy and economic assistance as the United States. Indeed, some countries might be particularly sensitive about becoming too closely associated with Washington, whereas they would not have the same inhibitions in relation to one or other of the European allies. A unilateral approach, therefore, would be far less attractive than one in which the Europeans and the United States coordinated their efforts through the NATO framework. Although this might appear to be placing too great a strain on the Alliance, the issues are already on the agenda. The outstanding question is whether they will be handled in a way which improves Alliance cohesion or undermines it. To argue in this way is not to advocate that the geographical responsibilities of the Alliance be extended: such a move is both undesirable and unnecessary. It is merely to suggest that NATO has an important, if informal, coordinating role, and that this will become increasingly important as the Europeans give more explicit consideration to the part they might play along with the Americans in dealing with problems outside the NATO area. This is certainly preferable to a division of labour in which Washington has exclusive responsibility for events elsewhere.

A third reason why it might be unwise to go so far concerns the situation in Europe itself. Although the Europeans need to exhibit far greater flexibility in relation to the size of the American presence in Europe, there is, as argued earlier, a minimum presence which needs to be maintained. To some degree at least, the symbol of the American commitment to Western Europe has become the substance. A graduated reduction of 50,000–100,000 military personnel in Europe could take place without necessarily undermining American credibility, but it would have to be accompanied by an explicit understanding that additional withdrawals would not be carried out. Moreover, in the light of the troop reductions, it would be undesirable to make radical reductions in American theatre nuclear weapons beyond those already announced. Simultaneous implementation of a troop reduction programme and a withdrawal of nuclear weapons could very easily give the wrong signals to both allies and adversary and create another crisis of confidence in NATO. A division of labour, therefore, could prove advantageous for the Alliance, so long as it did not go too far.

There are, of course, other ideas for a functional division of labour within the Alliance. Specialization of roles and responsibilities could bring considerable benefit. It has been argued, for example, that Britain could focus more on its maritime responsibilities, which take on a new significance if NATO plans on a long conventional war in Europe, and place less emphasis on the continental commitment. Although there is considerable promise in this kind of scheme, it would have far-reaching consequences for the allocation of resources among the services within particular nations, and might prove enormously difficult to implement. Nevertheless, as part of any comprehensive review of NATO's future, serious consideration would have to be given to such schemes, and to how they might be made more palatable and less disruptive at the national level.

Consideration could also be given to the suggestion that the post of SACEUR be filled by a European. This has been advocated most recently by Henry Kissinger, but the idea is an old one. It was proposed, for example, by Senator Frank Church in the mid-1960s as part of his argument that NATO be Europeanized.[5] The objection to it then was that SACEUR had special responsibility for nuclear targeting and a particularly important relationship with the American President, both of which would make it difficult for the post to be filled by a European. These objections still seem very persuasive, especially if one believes that the nuclear link with the United States is still the single most important element in European security. Kissinger, of course, gives little credence to this objection, since the whole thrust of his proposal is to minimize the nuclear risks to the United States of its commitment to Europe.

The best way of reducing these risks is not so much through a change of strategy as through a change of concepts. The Europeans probably have a much broader and more balanced notion of security than that held by the United States. The Europeans tend to regard security as something which can be promoted through cooperative measures based on mutual interests as well as through unilateral military efforts directed against the adversary. The United States, under President Reagan, has focused predominantly on military preparedness and, arguably, paid little more than lip service to dialogue and arms control. The unpublished but widely reported NATO study on East-West relations which was completed in the first half of 1984 went some way towards reconciling the divergent European and American attitudes, but still smacked of an aggregation of competing views rather than of an integration of complementary approaches.[6]

This suggests that the task for Western Europe in the 1980s and 1990s is to combine political accommodation and military strength in ways which make it less likely that the Russians will come and less likely that the Americans will go. Nevertheless, some cuts in the American presence might be permissible within a comprehensive reappraisal of roles and responsibilities, and of political and military strategies within NATO. In the final analysis, however, there will be a continuing need for a strong American military presence in Western Europe for the forseeable future. The continued deployment of American troops in Europe is in the interests of both the United States and Western Europe. It avoids confronting the Federal Republic with policy dilemmas which are better left dormant, and it reassures the Soviet Union. These are benefits which the advocates of American unilateralism and the proponents of European neutralism would do well to ponder. The existing framework of Atlantic relations may be untenable in some of its details, but the overall structure has a degree of resilience and stability which suggests that what is needed is a variation on an existing theme rather than an entirely new composition.

Notes

Chapter 1

1 H. Kissinger, 'A Plan to Reshape NATO', *Time*, 5 March 1984.
2 Quoted in *NATO Troop Withdrawals*, Hearings before the Committee on Foreign Relations, US Senate, 97th Congress, Second Session, 30 Nov. 1982 (Washington: Government Printing Office, 1982), p. 1. Hereafter cited as *NATO Troop Withdrawals*.
3 H. Pick, 'Pullout of Troops in Europe Rejected', *Guardian*, 9 March 1984.
4 M. Mansfield, *Congressional Record*, 23 Jan. 1970, p. S430.
5 H. Bull, 'European Self-Reliance and the Reform of NATO', *Foreign Affairs*, Vol. 61 (1983), No. 4, pp. 874–92.
6 See especially M. Bundy, G. F. Kennan, R. S. McNamara and G. Smith, 'Nuclear Weapons and the Atlantic Alliance', *Foreign Affairs*, Vol. 60 (1982), No. 4, pp. 753–68.
7 See K. Kaiser, S. Leber, A. Mertes and F. Schulze, 'Nuclear Weapons and the Preservation of Peace', *Foreign Affairs*, Vol. 60 (1982), No. 5, pp. 1157–70.
8 D. Calleo, *The Atlantic Fantasy* (Baltimore: Johns Hopkins University Press, 1970), p. 30.
9 The argument that risk-taking is a function of need rather than opportunity is developed in R. N. Lebow, 'Clear and Future Danger', in R. O'Neill and D. M. Horner (eds.), *New Directions in Strategic Thinking* (London: Allen and Unwin, 1981).
10 D. Nelson, 'Congress and US Troops in Germany', *Washington Times*, 15 March 1983.

Chapter 2

1 *Executive L, the North Atlantic Treaty*, Hearings before the Committee on Foreign Relations, US Senate, 81st Congress, First Session, Part I: Administration Witnesses, 27, 28 and 29 April, and 2 and 3

May, 1949, p. 47.

2 See S. R. Sloan, *Defense Burden-sharing: US Relations With NATO Allies and Japan*, Report No. 83-140F (Washington: Congressional Research Service, July 8, 1983), p. 46, for fuller details.

3 *NATO Troop Withdrawals*, p. 75.

4 The assumptions on which the Treaty was accepted by the Senate in 1949 are discussed more fully in P. Williams, *The Senate and US Troops in Europe* (London: Macmillan, in press).

5 See M. Bundy, *The Pattern of Responsibility* (Boston: Houghton Mifflin, 1952), p. 76.

6 This is one of the main themes of T. Ireland, *Creating the Entangling Alliance* (London: Aldwych Press, 1981).

7 *Ibid.*, pp. 190–5.

8 See, 'Growing Pressure in US to Cut Europe Garrisons', *The Times*, 23 Oct. 1963, and 'Eisenhower Urges Troop Cut Abroad', *New York Times*, 8 Nov. 1963.

9 See G. Treverton, *The Dollar Drain and American Forces in Germany* (Athens, Ohio: Ohio University Press, 1978), for a fuller discussion of this.

10 S. Sloan, 'Defence Burden-sharing in the Atlantic Alliance: The Role of the US Congress', *Europa-Archiv*, 25 Oct. 1981. See also S. Lunn, *Burden-sharing in NATO*, Chatham House Paper 18 (London: Routledge and Kegan Paul, for the Royal Institute of International Affairs, 1983), for a comprehensive analysis of the burden-sharing problem.

Chapter 3

1 W. Mako, *US Ground Forces and the Defence of Central Europe* (Washington: Brookings Institution, 1983), p. 1.

2 P. Bracken, *The Command and Control of Nuclear Forces* (New Haven and London: Yale University Press, 1983), pp. 136–7.

3 Of this figure, 322,957 were 'committed to NATO'. For a full breakdown, see S. R. Sloan, *Defence Burden Sharing: US Relations with NATO Allies and Japan*, p. 46.

4 These figures are based on Sloan, *op. cit.*, as well as C. Raj, *American Military in Europe* (New Delhi: ABC Publishing House, 1983) and *US Military Commitment to Europe*, Hearings Before the Ad Hoc Subcommittee of the Committee on Armed Services, House of Representatives, 93rd Congress, Second Session (Washington: Government Printing Office, 1974), p. 133.

5 Lawrence Eagleburger in *NATO Troop Withdrawals*, p. 10.

6 M. Bundy, 'The Future of Strategic Deterrence', *Survival*, Vol. 21 (1979) No. 6, pp. 268–72.

7 See A. Enthoven and W. Smith, *How Much is Enough?* (New York: Harper and Row, 1971). The reaction in the Pentagon to Enthoven's analysis is discussed by Raj, *The American Commitment to Europe*, pp. 102–40.

Notes

8   For a provocative assessment of the conventional balance, see
    J. J. Mearsheimer, 'Why the Soviets Can't Win Quickly in Central
    Europe', *International Security*, Vol. 7 (1982), No. 1, pp. 3–39.
9   *NATO Troop Withdrawals*, p. 10.
10 John Nott, quoted in *NATO Troop Withdrawals*, p. 1.
11 *Department of Defense Authorization for Appropriations for Fiscal
    Year 1982*, Hearings before the Committee on Armed Services on
    S.815 Part 1, 28 Jan. and 4 March, 1981, p. 61. The subsequent
    analysis is based on the figures provided on pp. 61–8.
12 R. Halloran, 'Europe Called Main US Arms Cost', *New York Times*,
    20 July 1984.
13 *Department of Defense Appropriations for Fiscal Year 1983*, Hear-
    ings Before a Subcommittee of the Committee on Appropriations,
    97th Congress, Second Session, Part II, pp. 221–2.
14 *Ibid*.
15 The study is referred to in *NATO Troop Withdrawals*, p. 71.

Chapter 4

1   Nunn Amendment. Quoted in *Congressional Quarterly Weekly
    Report*, Vol. 42, No. 25, 23 June 1984), p. 1480.
2   For a discussion and critique of this approach, see R. W. Komer,
    Maritime Strategy or Coalition Defence? (Cambridge, Mass.: Abt
    Books, 1984)..
3   L. Eagleburger, 'The Transatlantic Relationship — A Long-Term
    Perspective', Address Before the National Newspaper Association,
    Washington, 7 March 1984 (United States Information Service
    Official Text, 9 March 1984), p. 1.
4   *Ibid*., p. 2.
5   The National Bipartisan Commission on Central America, *Report*
    (Washington: Government Printing Office, 1984).
6   Quoted in Mako, *US Ground Forces and the Defence of Central
    Europe*, p. 65.
7   *Ibid*., p. 40.

Chapter 5

1   For an extremely useful overview of the debate, see the SIPRI
    publication, F. Blackaby, J. Goldblat and S. Lodgaard (eds.), *No-
    First-Use* (London and Philadelphia: Taylor and Francis, 1984).
2   See K. Kaiser, G. Leber, A. Mertes and F. Schulze, 'Nuclear Weapons
    and the Preservation of Peace'.
3   M. Howard, 'Reassurance and Deterrence: Western Defence in the
    1980s', *Foreign Affairs*, Vol. 61 (1982/3), No. 2, pp. 309–24.
4   See, for example, S. Canby, *The Alliance and Europe, part 4: Mili-
    tary Doctrine and Technology*, Adelphi Paper 109 (London: Inter-
    national Institute for Strategic Studies, 1975), and, more recently,
    S. Canby and I. Dörfer, 'More Troops, Fewer Missiles', *Foreign*

Policy, No. 53 (Winter 1983/4), pp. 3–17.

5 For a useful study exemplifying concern about non-provocation, see *Defence Without the Bomb: The Report of the Alternative Defence Commission* (London: Taylor and Francis, 1983).

6 I am grateful to Gert Krell of the International Institute for Strategic Studies for his comments about the criteria against which NATO's posture has to be assessed.

7 See Report of the European Security Study (ESECS), *Strengthening Conventional Deterrence in Europe: Proposals for the 1980s* (New York: St Martin's Press, 1983).

8 For a helpful discussion of the various proposals and the differences between them, see *Strategic Survey 1983–1984* (London: IISS, 1984), pp. 12–17.

9 F. O. Hampson, 'Groping For Technical Panaceas: The European Conventional Balance and Nuclear Stability', *International Security*, Vol. 8 (1983/4), No. 3, pp. 57–82.

10 B. R. Posen, 'Inadvertent Nuclear War? Escalation and NATO's Northern Flank', *International Security*, Vol. 7 (1982), No. 2, pp. 28–54.

11 T. C. Schelling, *Arms and Influence* (New Haven and London: Yale University Press, 1967), pp. 131–41.

12 As quoted in *Strategic Survey 1983–1984*, p. 16.

13 S. P. Huntington, 'Conventional Deterrence and Conventional Retaliation in Europe', *International Security*, Vol. 8 (1983/4), No. 3, pp. 32–56.

14 *Ibid.*, p. 42.

15 *Ibid.*, p. 56.

16 Mako, *US Ground Forces and the Defence of Central Europe*, p.32.

17 J. Keegan, quoted in *No-First-Use*; a report by the Union of Concerned Scientists (Cambridge, Mass., 1 Feb. 1983).

18 J. C. F. Tillson, 'The Forward Defence of Europe', ACIS Research Note 5 (UCLA Center for International and Strategic Affairs, 1979), pp. 1–15. This is quoted at some length in Mako, *US Ground Forces*, pp. 93–97.

19 *Surprise Attack* (Washington: Brookings Institution, 1982), p. 226.

20 J. H. Maurer and G. H. McCormick, 'Surprise Attack and Conventional Defence in Europe', *Orbis*, Vol. 27 (1983), No. 1, pp. 107–26.

21 P. Bracken, 'Urban Sprawl and NATO Defence', *Survival*, Vol. 18 (1976), No. 6, pp. 254–60.

22 Maurer and McCormick, 'Surprise Attack', p. 121.

23 L. Freedman, 'US Nuclear Weapons in Europe: Symbols, Strategy and Force Structure', in A. J. Pierre (ed.), *Nuclear Weapons in Europe*, pp. 45–74.

24 *The Command and Control of Nuclear Forces*, p. 165.

25 This is one of the main themes in *The Command and Control of Nuclear Forces*.

26 *Ibid.*, p. 129.

27 See R. Aron, *The Great Debate* (New York: Doubleday, 1965).
28 See, for example, J. W. Lewis and C. D. Blacker (eds.), *Next Steps in the Creation of an Accidental Nuclear War Prevention Center.* A special report of the Center for International Security and Arms Control, Stanford University (Oct. 1983), and S. Nunn and J. W. Warner, 'Reducing the Risk of Nuclear War', *Washington Quarterly*, Vol. 7 (1984), No. 2, pp. 3–7.

Chapter 6

1 See J. Record, 'Beyond NATO: New Military Directions for the United States', in J. Record and R. J. Hanks, *US Strategy at the Crossroads: Two Views* (Cambridge, Mass: Institute for Foreign Policy Analysis Inc., 1982), and H. A. Kissinger, 'A Plan to Re-shape NATO', *Time*, 5 March 1984.
2 *Report on Allied Contributions to the Common Defense* (March 1983), pp. 50–1.
3 I am indebted in the following paragraphs to the work on constraints on national defence efforts by David Greenwood, the Centre for Defence Studies, University of Aberdeen.
4 See G. Flynn, *The Internal Fabric of Western Security* (London: Croom Helm, 1981).
5 G. Krell, T. Risse-Kappen, and H. J. Schmidt, 'The No-First-Use Question in West Germany', in J. D. Steinbruner and L. V. Sigal (eds.), *Alliance Security: NATO and the No-First-Use Question* (Washington: Brookings Institution, 1983), p. 160.
6 *Ibid.*, p. 166.
7 Budget Speech of M. Charles Hernu, Minister of Defence, Before the Senate, 2 Dec. 1983, (London: French Embassy Press and Information Service, 10 January 1984).
8 Bracken, *The Command and Control of Nuclear Forces*, p. 164.
9 Schelling, *Arms and Influence*, p. 121, note 8.
10 The relationship between the warning and alert systems of the two superpowers is discussed more fully in Bracken, *The Command and Control of Nuclear Forces*.
11 B. Brodie, *Escalation and the Nuclear Option* (Princeton: Princeton University Press, 1966), p. 82.
12 See *Report on Allied Contributions to the Common Defence* (March 1983), p. 3. A useful discussion of the POMCUS issue is the Congressional Budget Office Background Paper *Strengthening NATO: POMCUS and other Approaches* (February 1979).
13 P. Bracken, 'The NATO Defence Problem', *Orbis*, Vol. 27 (1983), No. 1, p. 83.
14 L. Freedman, 'The United States Factor', in E. Moreton and G. Segal (eds.), *Soviet Strategy Toward Western Europe* (London: Allen and Unwin, 1984), p. 87.
15 A. Ulam, 'Western Europe is Soviet Union's Greatest Hope, Fear', *Post–Herald* (Birmingham, Alabama), 28 Oct. 1983.

Chapter 7

1 'A Plan to Reshape NATO', p. 16.
2 L. P. Brady and D. Fleck, 'Transatlantic Military Co-operation in Times of Crisis', *Atlantic Quarterly*, Vol. 2 (1984), No. 1, pp. 88–96.
3 Sloan, *Defence Burden-sharing: US Relations With NATO Allies and Japan*, p. 26.
4 Senator Claiborne Pell, 'Consensus, Public Support and the Future of the Alliance'. Statement at the North Atlantic Assembly, London, 19 Nov. 1982.
5 F. Church, 'Proposal to Europeanise NATO', *Congressional Record*, 7 March 1968, pp. S.2387–8.
6 A summary of the main points was issued. See 'Washington Statement on East–West Relations', issued by the North Atlantic Council on 31 May 1984. Also useful is N. Ashford, 'NATO Chiefs Look to Long Term', *The Times*, 2 June 1984.

Chatham House Papers

Chatham House Papers

Chatham House Papers provide full and up-to-date information on major issues of foreign policy, together with expert analysis. They are recognized as valuable and authoritative guides to some of the most important policy debates of the day. An annual subscription to six papers costs £22.00. We list current and forthcoming titles opposite. If you would like to subscribe, please complete the form below.

SUBSCRIPTION ORDER FORM

Please return this form to: or in USA or Canada to:

    Subscriptions,   Subscriptions,
    Routledge & Kegan Paul,   Routledge & Kegan Paul,
    Broadway House,   9 Park Street,
    Newtown Road,   Boston,
    Henley-on-Thames,   MA 02108, USA
    Oxon RG9 1EN, England

Please enter a subscription to Chatham House Papers (£22.00)

I enclose a cheque for _____
Please charge my Access/Barclaycard Number

Signature_____
Name _____
        (BLOCK CAPITALS)

Address _____
_____
_____